"God's perfect love is gentle; it is als will invade your heart as you read this for lukewarm Christianity and passio hunger will make you as insatiable for *Fire of Perfect Love* is more than a book; it's a gift."

Dutch Sheets, founder of Dutch Sheets Ministries and
GiveHim15.com

"In this book, Steven and Rene Springer will show you what it means to really be loved by the Father. In these pages, the revelation of the love of God is described with beauty, passion, and purpose. I recommend this book to all who want to dive deeper into what it really means to be an imitator of God."

Todd White, president and founder of Lifestyle Christianity

"*The Fire of Perfect Love* will revive your first love for God. Reading this book will open your heart to feel His love for you and in turn pour out your love for Him. Well written, passionate, and powerful."

Cindy Jacobs, co-founder of Generals International

"Steven and Rene Springer have a contagious zeal and love for the Lord. This book is for every Christian who is in pursuit of a deeper, more intimate walk with the Lord and wants to make history as God's firebrand in this generation. Read it and you, too, will catch the fire of perfect love."

Lou Engle, president of Lou Engle Ministries

"My dear friends Steven and Rene Springer have tasted and seen that the 'fire of His perfect love' is both majestic and transforming, and yet so approachable. Go on a prophetic journey with these authentic revivalists."

James W. Goll, founder of God Encounters Ministries
and GOLL Ideation LLC

"I have known Steven and Rene Springer for many years and have observed them consistently walking in love. *The Fire of Perfect Love* unpacks the most important topic in the Bible—LOVE—and this book is truly a gift of inspiration to all who read it."

Patricia King, author, minister, media producer, and host;
founder of Patricia King Ministries

"Steven and Rene perfectly describe the process of walking through His plan and purpose for your life, enabling you to fulfill your

God-ordained destiny. The revelation in this book has a transformative power and is something we all need. God's love never fails."

Apostle Tim Sheets, Tim Sheets Ministries

"*The Fire of Perfect Love* is a breath of fresh air. As the Body of Christ, we need to go deeper into Him and into His love. Our identity as sons and daughters of God grants us the authority to keep on with the task He has set before us."

Juanita Cercone, legal director, Enlace

"*The Fire of Perfect Love* will set you ablaze with passion to know the Lord more deeply and intimately. As I read, I could sense the anointing on every page. This book will empower you with a fresh revelation of God's love that will change your spiritual life forever."

Jane Hamon, author and senior pastor, Vision Church
at Christian International

"*The Fire of Perfect Love* is an invitation to encounter a true revival of the heart. It unleashes the call to dream with God, live from the supernatural realms, and believe for more than we ever thought possible. This book is a true experience of the ultimate pursuit and power of God's love."

Jodi Hannah, president and producer
of Streaming House Entertainment

"Steven and Rene are some of the most love-filled pastors I have ever met. They are full of enthusiasm for God and full of love for people, so their ministry is full of miracles."

Elder Jason Hu, executive elder and senior pastor of Abundant
Favor Church, Taiwan; deputy chancellor of Taiwan Agape
International Leadership Institute

"Steven and Rene Springer are priceless servants used by God. Their ministries manifest the power of God, as well as glorify the name of God globally. I surely believe this book will make your life different."

Pastor Joseph Wang, founder of FHL Team

"Steven and Rene are living proof that the agape love of God that He has poured into our hearts is real and works now, today. This book is their testimony of this ever-fiery, ever-heart-gripping, and ever-life-changing love of God."

Zoran Spasovski, president of Christian Center Churches
in Macedonia, Grace Amazing

"No one since early Salvation Army leaders and old-school Methodists have articulated the revelation of perfect love as powerfully until Steven and Rene. *The Fire of Perfect Love* will lead you into deeper intimacy with the Lord as you seek your own encounter with the flame of His love."

Lance Wallnau, CEO of Lance Learning Group

"Steven and Rene have divinely appeared in my life at crossroads moments. My life will never be the same. I have been a witness to the power and fire that they encounter moment by moment—it is available for each of us."

David L. Cook, Ph.D., author and executive producer
of *Seven Days in Utopia*

"If the Bible is God's love letter to the world, Steven and Rene's book is a key to deciphering it. Beautifully explaining God's love in its fullness, they guide the reader through practical reflection and powerful declarations to set ablaze the fire of perfect love within each believer's heart."

Maksim Asenov, author, entrepreneur, spiritual leader,
and founder of Awakening Church, Sofia, Bulgaria

"*The Fire of Perfect Love* is the best and easiest-to-understand book I've ever read on love. Steven and Rene's moving personal stories are a road map for navigating tough times. I absolutely love this book and encourage everyone to read it!"

Camp Chan, founder of the Zebulun Apostolic Centre–Hong Kong

"Steven and Rene Springer are anointed leaders whose lives have been marked by the fire of God's perfect love. In this book, you will journey into God's fiery love for you! Get ready to be recalibrated and ignited into His purposes. It is time to gaze and GO!"

Jonathan and Sharon Ngai, co-founders of Radiance
International and Hollywood House of Prayer

"All we need is found in Jesus, who is LOVE. This book is more than teaching, it is an impartation. I encourage everyone to read and digest deeply. I believe these words have the power to leave readers forever changed."

Faytene Grasseschi, TV show host, author, revivalist

"Steven and Rene have blessed the Body of Christ with some tremendous truths. It is a fiery love that brings passion and purpose to your life, establishing you in unshakable faith that will enable you to fulfill God's call and destiny for your life."

Dr. Bill Hamon, author and founder of Christian International Apostolic Network

"In *The Fire of Perfect Love*, Steven and Rene take us back to the heart of the matter—that it's not about what we're seeking, but who we're seeking. This alone is transformational!"

Arleen Westerhof, co-lead pastor and co-founder of God's Embassy Amsterdam, co-founder of European Prophetic Council

"Steven and Rene's stories of divine encounter will inspire you and set your heart on fire! You will see the reality of God's nearness and be positioned to encounter the glorious fire of His love. Read this book with a wide-open heart for God to encounter you with a new depth of His love and impart His living flame into you."

Matt Sorger, author, prophetic minister, spiritual mentor, transformational coach

"*The Fire of Perfect Love* is for anyone who desires to encounter the love of God and longs to draw closer to this purifying, transforming love. This perfect, fiery love of God has clearly transformed Steven and Rene, which is evident in the way they love and serve others."

Pattie Mallette, producer, speaker, and author of *Nowhere but Up: The Story of Justin Bieber's Mom*

"I'm convinced that God wants to take you from a Christianity of religious rituals to holy obsession. *The Fire of Perfect Love* carries a prophetic theme that heaven is emphasizing in this hour. It will revolutionize your life and is sure to be a classic."

Sean Smith, author and co-director of Sean and Christa Smith Ministries

"*The Fire of Perfect Love* is a powerful revelation of the ferocious passion of God for His people. Being convinced of God's affection breaks the chains of the enemy and launches us into the purposes of God. Freedom and destiny will be released to many through these pages!"

Shane Holden, senior pastor at First Free Church, Onalaska, Wisconsin

THE
FIRE OF
PERFECT
LOVE

INTIMACY WITH GOD FOR A LIFE OF
PASSION, PURPOSE, AND UNSHAKABLE FAITH

STEVEN AND RENE SPRINGER

Chosen

a division of Baker Publishing Group
Minneapolis, Minnesota

© 2023 by Steven and Rene Springer

Published by Chosen Books
Minneapolis, Minnesota
www.chosenbooks.com

Chosen Books is a division of
Baker Publishing Group, Grand Rapids, Michigan

Printed in the United States of America

ISBN 978-0-8007-6328-2 (trade paper)
ISBN 978-1-4934-4110-5 (ebook)
ISBN 978-0-8007-6336-7 (casebound)

Library of Congress Cataloging-in-Publication Control Number: 2023007610

Unless otherwise indicated, Scripture quotations are from the New King James Version®. Copyright © 1982 by Thomas Nelson. Used by permission. All rights reserved.

Scripture quotations marked AMP are from the Amplified® Bible (AMP), copyright © 2015 by The Lockman Foundation. Used by permission. www.Lockman.org

Scripture quotations marked AMPC are from the Amplified® Bible (AMPC), copyright © 1954, 1958, 1962, 1964, 1965, 1987 by The Lockman Foundation. Used by permission. www.Lockman.org

Scripture quotations marked ESV are from The Holy Bible, English Standard Version® (ESV®), copyright © 2001 by Crossway, a publishing ministry of Good News Publishers. Used by permission. All rights reserved. ESV Text Edition: 2016

Scripture quotations marked MSG are taken from *THE MESSAGE*, copyright © 1993, 2002, 2018 by Eugene H. Peterson. Used by permission of NavPress. All rights reserved. Represented by Tyndale House Publishers, Inc.

Scripture quotations marked NIV are from THE HOLY BIBLE, NEW INTERNATIONAL VERSION®, NIV® Copyright © 1973, 1978, 1984, 2011 by Biblica, Inc.® Used by permission. All rights reserved worldwide.

Scripture quotations marked NLT are taken from the Holy Bible, New Living Translation, copyright © 1996, 2004, 2015 by Tyndale House Foundation. Used by permission of Tyndale House Publishers, Inc., Carol Stream, Illinois 60188. All rights reserved.

Scripture quotations marked TPT are from The Passion Translation®. Copyright © 2017, 2018 by Passion & Fire Ministries, Inc. Used by permission. All rights reserved. ThePassionTranslation.com.

Scriptures marked VOICE are taken from the THE VOICE (The Voice): Scripture taken from THE VOICE ™. Copyright© 2008 by Ecclesia Bible Society. Used by permission. All rights reserved.

Cover design by LOOK Design Studio

23   24   25   26   27   28   29   7   6   5   4   3   2   1

We dedicate this book to Holy Spirit,
who set us on fire with perfect love and
placed a longing inside us that nothing other
than the love of the Lord can satisfy.

To our amazing family
and our Global Presence tribe,
who have loved, prayed, and supported
us as we have written this book.
We love you all dearly and are
so thankful for you.

To the legacy of love expressed through
our beloved mothers who have passed on,
Patsy Ann Springer and Beverly Jean Wolfe,
and our future generations of children,
grandchildren, and great grandchildren.

To the lovers of Jesus who will read this book
and be set ablaze to display the beauty of the
Lord to a world desperate for the revelation
of what the fire of perfect love looks like.

CONTENTS

FOREWORD

The Fire of Perfect Love invites you to enter a world where you are loved unconditionally and where you can discover who you truly are in the eyes of God. It is a journey that can bring healing, freedom, and a deep sense of purpose. At the heart of this book is the truth that God loves you with endless, fiery, and perfect love. This love is not dependent on anything you have done or achieved, but is yours simply because of who God is. It seeks to draw you closer to Him, transform you from the inside out, and empower you to co-laborer Him in His redemptive work in the world.

As you read this book, you will discover that the fire of God's love has the power to set you free from everything that troubles you. It can heal the wounds of your past, give you hope for your future, and fill your present with joy and peace. It can restore emotional wholeness; increase your influence in your family, city, and workplace; and give you the confidence to live a life of purpose and meaning.

The journey to experiencing God's love on a deeper level can be a daunting one. We may feel unworthy, unloved, or even skeptical about the idea of a God who loves us unconditionally. But let me assure you, His love is real, and it is available to you.

One of the most beautiful things about the love of God is that it is personal. It is not a generic love that is the same for everyone, but a unique and individual love tailored specifically to you. This means that as you experience it more deeply, you will discover aspects of your identity and purpose that you may never have realized before. You will begin to see yourself as God sees you, and you will be empowered to live out the fullness of who you were created to be.

God's love is not just a theoretical concept; it is a tangible reality that we can experience every day. When we encounter it, we are transformed from the inside out. The fire of His love burns away all that is not of Him, and we are left with a renewed sense of purpose and direction.

Steven and Rene Springer are precious friends and a dynamic couple who minister together. Their example of living a life of love has impacted our lives. Many can testify how the Springers have opened heaven's doors and imparted this message of love. You hold in your hands the fruit of their lives laid down in love for God. Get ready to experience God's love on a deeper level. It is a journey that will require vulnerability and openness, but it is a journey worth taking.

As you read these pages, you will be invited to reflect on your own experiences and to discover how God's love is different from any other love you have ever known. You will be challenged to let go of any barriers or misconceptions you may have and embrace it wholeheartedly. Through these powerful personal testimonies of God's fiery love, you will see firsthand how God can change cold hearts into a furnace burning bright with eternal love. Jesus is glad you are reading this book!

You are about to discover how to tap into the never-ending source of God's love. You will learn how to let go of the things that have been holding you back from experiencing His love fully. You will be empowered to know who you really are in His eyes, and this knowledge will give you the confidence to live in emotional wholeness and freedom. And you will find comfort in the intensity of God's love. It is not passive or distant, but it is active and present and with us every moment of every day. No matter what you may be going through, His love is always there to comfort, encourage, and empower you.

As you go deeper into His love, you will discover what you were created for. You will find that you are not just a passive recipient, but you are a co-laborer with Him. Steven and Rene writing this book together so beautifully symbolize the co-laboring of the Bride and Jesus, the Bridegroom, writing history together and bringing the revelation of God's burning heart to the world!

You have a unique role to play in His Kingdom, and His love will empower you to fulfill that role. As you experience God's love on a deeper level, you will also find that your influence will increase. You will have a greater impact on your family, your city, and your workplace. Your relationships will be transformed, and you will be a beacon of hope and love to those around you.

I know you're going to enjoy this book! And may the fire of perfect love burn bright in us until all fear is cast out from our lives forever!

Brian Simmons
Passion & Fire Ministries
The Passion Translation Project

INTRODUCTION

Encountering the Fire of Perfect Love

We have had the privilege of discipling thousands of people over the years. The number one factor that has brought the most personal growth and transformation is a person's willingness to receive and yield to the fire of God's perfect love.

For many years, while we lived in Madison, Wisconsin, we had a house of prayer called The Furnace on one of the biggest party streets near the University of Wisconsin campus. It was an old, small laundromat that we transformed into a fiery place of God's presence fueled by worship, prayer, and creative arts. This dedicated place of God's presence in the heart of our city was an outpost from which teams filled with His presence would go out, bringing the love and power of God to touch people on the streets.

The Furnace was surrounded by university housing, a bus station, and other old buildings. From the outside there was little indication as to what was happening inside. This made for some interesting adventures, and we never knew who would walk through the doors. An on-fire believer? Someone active in the occult? A homeless person asking for resources? Someone addicted to drugs? Someone seeking to experience God? Or a college student walking in with a load of laundry? To those carrying baskets of dirty clothes, we had fun responding, "This isn't a laundromat anymore, but we may be able to help you with a different kind of laundry!"

One thing was certain: Whoever walked in would feel God's presence tangibly. Even those without the language to describe it would use words like *peace, warmth*, or *a presence*. And for those who stuck around, it was only a matter of time before they encountered the transformative fire of God's perfect love.

One such time was with a man we will call Roger, who had been homeless for a long time. He often came in and hung out with us. He became our friend, and through him we learned quite a bit about the homeless community. He was a leader and cared deeply for them; in a sense, he was pastoring his community. We provided some resources to help care for and sustain them, but what happened to Roger after he experienced the tangible fire of God's love was transformational.

We will never forget that night at The Furnace. In the midst of worship, Roger was sweating profusely. He was perched on the edge of his seat, his eyes really big with a tinge of concern in them. It was evident that God's presence was encountering him in a way that he clearly did not understand. We walked over to Roger, offered him a bottle of water, and asked what was going on.

"I'm not sure," he replied. "My whole body is on fire. Is this a bad fire, like what's in hell?"

"Oh, no, Roger," we said. "What you're experiencing is the fire of God's love for you and His desire to burn away hindrances that keep you from receiving more of His love. God wants to bring forth the gold in you."

After more explanation, he sighed with relief and sank back in his chair. He was still sweating but remained in a receiving posture for the rest of the evening.

From that night on, the fruit of Roger's encounter with God was evident, and his life started to change rapidly. Soon he was able to get a job, as he could now see and believe that he had valuable gifts to contribute to society. His name, which had been on a long waiting list for subsidized housing, "suddenly" came to the top of the list, and he was able to secure an apartment after years of living on the streets. God's perfect love was leading him out of the fear of never being good enough and into the safety of God's love and acceptance.

Roger began to bring others who were homeless to The Furnace. Not all were ready to receive from God's presence, but in the ones who were, we saw rapid change, most often in their ability to work again. We believe that is because the fire helped burn the "scales" off their spiritual eyes so they could feel valued and seen by God, and, in turn, see themselves as having something of value to contribute.

Roger's heart continued to expand, and we became family to him as he found community in God's house. Whenever the doors of The Furnace opened, he was there. He learned to find comfort in the fire.

Roger was once homeless and poor, but aren't we all without Jesus? All people without Jesus, in all walks of life, are poor in spirit and without their eternal home. We have had the privilege to minister to down-and-outers, up-and-outers, and everyone in between—leaders of nations, heads of industries, neighbor next door. We have seen the fiery presence of God's

Spirit overtake corporate board meetings, consume villages in Africa, sweep through entire government offices, light up a movie set with heavenly revelation, and move through children in profound ways. We are in an all-saints movement, and God is setting apart His people and marking them with the fire of His perfect love.

In the forever-changing world all around us, we can be certain of one thing: the matchless, unfailing, and unending fiery love of God. God loves you because He wants to, not because you have earned it or deserve it. He loves you because He *is* love! God's fire of perfect love is unconditional, unfailing, and always available.

Often we function from our own strength and our own ability to serve Him, but Jesus has something completely different in mind. It is all about love—a burning, fascinated heart captivated by the amazing God who created you in His image to do great and mighty things in His name for His Kingdom, a co-laborer with Him forever.

You can know who you really are and experience the sense of being His child, knowing the lavish love of God, walking like Him, talking like Him, loving like Him, all rooted in being with Him—not just knowing about Him, but knowing Him intimately. This book will help you to know what it is to lean on your Beloved rather than on your own understanding.

We have written *The Fire of Perfect Love* to:

- reveal God's passionate pursuit of you;
- invite you to know the depth of His love and receive its fullness, so you can realize the fullness of who you are and what you were created for;
- bring forth boldness in you as fear is cast out;

- impart grace to you to embrace the flame that removes hindrances from receiving more of His love. This will transform you from the inside out and increase your sphere of influence: family, workplace, community. Everywhere your feet go, the Kingdom of God is at hand!

The fire of God's love and His pursuit of you will not let up until it brings you into the fullness of His perfect love. This book will help you get there. We have lived out the words on these pages and found them true, in our lives and in the lives of those God has entrusted to us to disciple through sharing life together.

As you yield to Holy Spirit, the increase of His purifying fire will burn up whatever hinders you from receiving more of His perfect love, revealing who you truly are. Beloved, stay in the flame. Find comfort in the intensity of His love. The fire of God's perfect love is unveiling your identity as God's glorious son or daughter.

Visual and/or audio materials that correspond with each chapter are available on our website, www.globalpresence.com/Perfect Love.

ONE

Love Is the Goal

Three things will last forever—faith, hope, and love—and the greatest of these is love. Let love be your highest goal!

1 Corinthians 13:13–14:1 NLT

Steven

One night as I was feasting on the revelation of God's Word concerning love, I fell asleep with 1 Corinthians 13 on my mind and in my heart.

We had been seeing people in ministry burn out, get caught in extramarital affairs, and lose their families. I had been reading biographies of God's generals of the faith used powerfully throughout history, whose lives did not end well because of their lack of character and communion with the Lord. Their first love for God ceased being first—and that is not what I wanted in my future. So for more than a month I had been reading

1 Corinthians 13, what many call "the love chapter," seeking the Lord for fresh understanding.

Early in the morning I was awakened by the audible voice of the Lord calling me by name. A sweet, thunderous voice of love, affection, and weight filled me with awe. I looked over at Rene to see if she heard it, too, but she remained in a deep sleep. He said my name *Steven* three times. It reverberated throughout my entire being. I was awake and alert.

The Lord asked me a question: *Are you serious about 1 Corinthians 13 and the revelation of My fiery, perfect love?*

Even though I was confident in my response, I found it hard to speak because I was gripped by the fear of the Lord. But my longing broke through, and with a slight quiver in my voice, I answered, "Yes, Lord, I long to know this love with my complete being. Would You show me?"

Immediately the whole room was filled with the smell of incense. The room grew hot, and I saw two angels, faces glowing with glory and with eyes of love. Their garments were glistening white. Their wings were on fire, orange in color, and roaring like a bonfire.

My heart was beating fast. I was in complete awe of what I was seeing, hearing, and sensing. I was encountering the God of the universe! I could feel my breath being caught away in the weight of His glory. I thought I would die. I had to keep wiping the tears streaming from my eyes.

One of the angels said, "Are you ready for the fire of heavenly love?"

I responded with excitement and wonder, "Yes, I have to know this love. I won't be satisfied unless I do!"

The angels began to flap their massive wings vigorously. It sounded like a roaring jet engine, and the flames on their wings changed from orange to blue, the flames now consuming their wings.

There was a change in the atmosphere, and the room was filled with a flowery fragrance. My whole being was surrounded by an overwhelming presence of love and peace. It was as if love was being poured into me, consuming me. Overcome with joy, I began to weep and smile at the same time. I was being transformed.

Then the room was filled with light and the flames of fiery affections from heaven. I knew that as fiery love consumed me, it was a message I was to carry to the ends of the earth, bringing the awakening and reality of the fire of perfect love. I knew this quest was to be a forever journey, from now into eternity.

As the angels began to transition back behind the veil of the unseen realm, the fragrance and glory remained in the room for a while, but I was able to breathe normally again. The *shalom* of heaven brought comfort to the depths of my being as I began to process all that had happened.

Rene woke up, and I shared with her everything that had happened in this encounter.

The apostle Paul had incredible insight and experiences with God's love. It is what compelled him after his conversion. He chose to write the love chapter in between his instructions on ministry and the gifts of the Spirit in 1 Corinthians 12 and 14.

Love is to be at the center of how we live and what we do. What Paul wrote has become my motivation for all of life: "Go after a life of love as if your life depended on it—because it does" (1 Corinthians 14:1 MSG). We are designed by love and for love, and we are on this quest of discovery from now until eternity.

The Distortion of Love

In a world riddled with conflicting messages and opinions, we have become entrapped in *Who is right?* rather than *What is right?* in the eyes of God. We are often more in love with our own opinions, convinced they are right, than we are with God and learning to love through Him. We are missing the reality and power of love.

History has a way of repeating itself. Nations prosper and then lose sight of God, becoming prideful, trusting in their own efforts and putting many other things before God. When we lose sight of God, His image becomes distorted, and a distorted image of God produces distorted expressions of love. Today these include:

- Lack of loyalty and commitment in relationships. Rejection and separation, instead of unconditional love, are our go-to reactions. A breakup, instead of forgiveness and reconciliation, is the response to unhappiness or "irreconcilable differences."

- Little to no real intimacy. People connect through texting and social media, but our growing isolation leads to depression and suicide.

- Abusive and immoral sexual behavior. Cravings of the flesh replace the connection of the heart. We have lost sight of the beauty of sex in the context of marriage. People pursue and justify hurtful sexual deviance instead of cherishing what God designed as an expression of pleasure and comfort.

- Affluence and the pursuit of external wealth. Riches have eliminated the need for God, and we turn to possessions to fill our need for love, acceptance, value, and influence.

- Defining people by their behaviors instead of their God-given identity. This leads to shame and guilt instead of joy and freedom.

- Family dysfunction. Chaos feels like love because of generational patterns, strongholds, or simple ignorance. Parents do not know how to discipline in love, and leave the raising of their children to "professionals" instead of taking their own rightful place.

- Racism, sexism, division, and violence. Vengeance is considered justice, and rebellion against authority is celebrated.

Looking for Love

It was this distortion of love that got us searching. We met in the modeling industry in our twenties. We did not know Jesus. As a model, Rene saw a business opportunity and started her own agency, contracting models and talent all over the world. Steven was one of those models who received international contracts. An agent dating one of the models—not ethical, but it is how our relationship started.

We began living the so-called dream in an exciting, fast-paced lifestyle—travel, adventure, lucrative contracts, who's-who parties, nightclubs, being seen, admired, and sought after. But the taste of success left us with an insatiable appetite for more, in a downward spiral of discontent. The glamorous fast lane was leading to a dead end. True love and fulfillment escaped us. We were looking for love, acceptance, and purpose in all the wrong places.

What was life about? Why were we here? Was there more to life than this? These aching questions, as well as our broken pasts and misrepresentations of love, finally led us to the end of ourselves and into an encounter with the perfect love of our Savior.

God pursued both of us at the same time, while we were halfway around the world from each other. Steven had a demonstrative encounter while in Barcelona, Spain, on a modeling contract. Rene had someone from the industry share Jesus with her on a business trip to Hollywood, which opened her heart to the possibility of God.

When we came back together, we did not share our experiences with each other, but started seeking God individually and secretly, until some unusual circumstances provoked us to share with each other. Then we began to seek God together.

At the end of the evening at a Christmas party in a relative's living room, not only did we receive Jesus as our personal Lord and Savior, but we received the baptism of Holy Spirit and fire.

Steven describes this experience as a big ball of fire hitting him in the stomach, consuming his entire being, dropping him to his knees, and enabling him to speak in a language he did not know. Rene's experience was just as significant but less demonstrative. God spoke to her in a still, small voice—a spark that would eventually become a full flame. It was the beginning of a life full of wonder, continued encounters, and great adventures.

God is faithful to encounter people right where they are, in ways that best meet their personalities. One thing for certain—if it were not for the firepower of Holy Spirit, it would have been really hard for us to come out from destructive patterns and begin the journey of truly being set apart.

Coming out of our earlier life was not easy. You expect the world not to get love right—denying God, distorting His image, embracing other gods. But the Church has also missed the mark. Consider how we still get trapped in the following:

- Religious duty, measured by what we do rather than who we are. This has produced a lack of intimacy, burnout, doing rather than being. Many of us feel we must clean ourselves up first rather than come to God as we are and allow His perfect love to change us.

- Fear-based Christianity. Instead of walking in the fear of the Lord—honoring and respecting God in His majesty—we fear others and their opinions. We base love on performance, and are plagued by striving, shame, and guilt.

- Forgetting our first love. We entertain other lovers, putting people and things before God—which is idolatry.

- An orphan spirit. Even when we confess that Jesus has forgiven our sins, we still relate to God as sinners instead of saints, striving to serve Him to try to feel accepted and loved.

- Prayerlessness. We see prayer as a religious duty rather than an intimate connection. We pray because we want something from God, rather than simply longing to connect with Him.

- Carnal living. Many who call themselves Christians live no differently from the world, even though God calls us to be set apart as holy.

- Functioning as an organization rather than a living organism. At church we focus on programs and performance rather than encountering God's presence in our midst.

If the Church were living and thriving in love, the world would want what we have. God gave us the greatest love story ever written: the Bible. The Bible reveals to us that "God is love" (1 John 4:8). The Father sent the Son on the greatest rescue mission of all time, for the sake of love. Holy Spirit invites us into this incredible love story, not to study it for knowledge's sake, but to experience it for love's sake.

The extravagance of God's love cannot be confined to the pages of a book or the structure of a church service. The Bible and spiritual gatherings are meant to reveal God, not to contain Him. God takes great pleasure in having His love story continue to be expressed on the pages of human hearts. We are described in 2 Corinthians 3:3 as "living letters written by Christ, not with ink but by the Spirit of the living God—not carved onto stone tablets but on the tablets of tender hearts." We were made to experience love in a way that transforms us from the inside out, becoming the very testimony of God on the earth.

The goal of human existence is to know and love God. So why would love not be the greatest battlefield the enemy is attempting to conquer? How we define and relate to love determines how we grow in love, portray love, and give love to those we know and to the world around us. We must pursue love. And we must pursue the God of love.

Compelled by Love to Follow

We were created in God's image, and He is the very essence of love. We are instructed to go after a life of love, making it our goal. First Corinthians 14:1 (AMP) says, "Pursue [this] love [with eagerness, make it your goal]."

Every one of us, regardless of whether we know Jesus, is created for God's good pleasure, to experience His delight. This is why Jesus said that loving God is the first and greatest commandment: "Love the Lord your God with all your heart and with all your soul and with all your mind and with all your strength" (Mark 12:30 NIV).

Love has the power to change the world, but few have the courage to go after love with everything within them. Jesus knew this when He began His ministry, starting a revolution with just twelve disciples. He saw beyond their imperfections, spoke to the courage in their hearts, and called them into greatness. Jesus said two simple words, "Follow Me," and the disciples left everything to follow Him.

Let's stop and think about this for a moment. Jesus said simply, "Follow Me." He did very little vision-casting for them. He definitely did not give them a clear mission statement. No retirement plan. No guarantees. The disciples had no idea what they were signing up for. Their seemingly impulsive response to chase this Prophet and Teacher who had burst onto the scene was not a rational decision by any means.

What in the world compelled them to such radical action? Was it the resonance of His voice? Flashes of fire in His eyes, perhaps? A hope, a promise that stirred within them? Or could it be, in that moment of invitation, that they encountered perfect love in such a profound way that their fear was dispelled and they felt alive and ready to risk it all?

Perfect Love is also knocking on the door of your heart with an invitation to fall in love—or more deeply in love—with the One who is Love.

Who Is Your Finish Line?

Steven

I remember a season early in our walk with the Lord when Rene and I were ministering and traveling all over. We had started a worship and ministry band, traveling in our region and to the nations. Our slogan was "Music with a Message, Fueling Fire for the Masses." We were invited into multiple denominations—from Lutheran to Catholic to charismatic, and from church events to secular community events—bringing the message of the Kingdom.

As we went, we saw great fruit, with revival breaking out and many coming to know Jesus for the first time. We saw healing and miracles regularly. The cry of our hearts was "Here we are, Lord, send us!" We longed to minister wherever the Lord opened doors. We were consumed by zeal since He had pulled us out of the mire and brought us into His marvelous light.

At the same time, we were part of a rapidly growing evangelistic church. One week a guest speaker shared a message about running the race with endurance, posing this question: "Who is at your finish line? Is your influence for Jesus your finish line? Or is Jesus Himself your finish line?"

A weight of glory came over me and I sensed Holy Spirit touch my heart gently. I saw in a moment that Jesus was not my finish line. He was not first place in my heart. I was going, going, and going, and doing, doing, and doing all kinds of things for Him. I was serving God sincerely with everything—time, money, and gifts. But my works were based on the second commandment of loving my neighbors, not the first commandment of loving God. My pursuit was not His face. It reminded me of what Jesus said to the church at Ephesus: "I have this against you: you have abandoned the passionate love you had for me at the beginning" (Revelation 2:4 TPT).

The weight of Holy Spirit's loving conviction made me realize that I needed to recalibrate my priorities and love God with my complete being or else burn out. As the loving presence of the Lord was on me, I began to weep and pour out my heart to Him. I repented for not making Him my top pursuit.

Grace and love filled my heart, and I was restored as one who could just be—be in His presence, be loved, be refreshed, be a child of the Most High God, and just be me!

We wander away from the reality of God's perfect love and keeping Him in first place. But when we repent, we turn around so we are gazing on His face once again, beholding the eyes of fiery passion. As we do, we see His joy, His smile, His delight, and His arms open wide, receiving us and anyone who will turn to His loving presence.

Let's look again at Jesus' words from Mark 12:

> "You are to love the Lord Yahweh, your God, with a passionate heart, from the depths of your soul, with your every thought, and with all your strength. This is the great and supreme commandment. And the second is this: 'You must love your neighbor in the same way you love yourself.' You will never find a greater commandment than these."
>
> verses 30–31 TPT

There is a recalibration going on right now with God's people. The first commandment will be first once again in His people. We must go after lives of love as if our lives depend on it, because they do. When we talk about making love the goal, we need to understand that love is not about an emotion.

It is about experiencing a Person, God Himself. When we encounter His amazing, perfect love, and when we make love the goal in everything we do, we will see God for who He really is.

In the above Scripture, there are four dimensions with which we are to love the Lord our God: the heart, soul, mind, and strength—everything we are. There is no way we can love Him unless His love was poured out on us first. He showed His love for us in that "while we were still sinners, Christ died for us" (Romans 5:8 NIV). Jesus first loved us with His complete being, and from this revelation we are empowered to love Him back with everything we are.

Humans have lived many centuries without understanding the fullness of God's love as expressed in Jesus, but now God is recalibrating His people so we align our hearts with the first commandment. He must be our goal and first pursuit.

Discovering Perfect Love

Rene

In our honest pursuit of first love, we will discover areas in our lives that are hindering us. In a time of prayer, listening, and journaling, I was sharing with the Lord my heart and how perfectionism was robbing me of enjoying life. I asked Him for freedom from it.

As I listened for His guidance, I was surprised by the way He responded. He started by affirming my longing to be perfected.

What?!

He shared with me that my longing to be perfected is from Him! But the way in which He would fulfill this longing would be through His love not fear. He continued to reveal that the root of perfectionism is fear—fear of not being good enough—which is really a form of pride, because I am making it about my works, not His. It is His perfect love that will perfect me, He said, not fear.

Was freedom as simple as receiving more of God's love, and fear would go away?

> There is no fear in love, but perfect love casts out fear. For fear has to do with punishment, and whoever fears has not been perfected in love.
>
> 1 John 4:18 ESV

I began reciting this life-giving Scripture out loud over and over while posturing my heart to receive. I turned it into a prayer, declaring, "Fear no longer has a place in my heart because perfect love now fills it." I repented, coming out of agreement with the operation of fear in my life, and forbidding the punishment it brings from affecting me.

As I began to believe that my love, even weak love, was enough, my mind and emotions started to shift. Loving God will always be enough. We must resist religious mindsets that try to complicate the simplicity of loving God and being loved by Him, which is enough!

We are applauded for perfectionism along with our achievements, but in the process, we are robbed of joy in life. "Achiever" is high on my own personality profile, so I am not repenting of who God created me to be; but it is the driving force behind it that I must be aware of. I am learning that it is possible to be a high achiever with a spirit of excellence, free from the bondage of perfectionism, and that our achievements can be motivated by love rather than fear.

There is freedom in the revelation that, although God is perfect, He has chosen weak, imperfect people to receive His perfect love and through whom to release it. Our process of growing in love will be messy yet beautiful, risky yet steady, exhausting yet exhilarating, satisfying yet longing for more, confusing at times yet the only thing that truly makes sense in life. The beauty of God's love is that He is patient with us and enjoys relating to us in each stage of our discovery.

God Is Good and He Is for Us!

We have had the privilege of co-laboring with God in releasing many miracles: blind eyes opening, a glass eye being replaced by a brand-new eye in the socket, a massive face tumor dissolving and being replaced by beautiful new skin, a paralyzed person walking—and the list goes on. Our privilege is not only to do the same works as Jesus, but to equip the saints for the "greater works" (see John 14:12). As we impart the gift of faith in equipping the Body of Christ, we find that the biggest hindrances to healing are unbelief and accepting God's love.

In order for love to be the goal in our faith walk, we must be convinced of God's love. Evil things that happen in the world are the result of the curse and Satan's plan of destruction of everything God loves. We must resist agreement with the accuser, who accuses God, accuses us, and gets us to accuse each other. Let's give credit where credit is due. Satan comes to kill, steal, and destroy. God comes to bring life, restoration and healing.

God is good and He is for us. The Bible asks, "If God is for us, who can be against us?" (Romans 8:31 NIV). This does not mean there is not warfare. We are in a real battle daily. There is a devil who hates you with a passion. But there is a God who has

34

an even greater passion, which is you. He loves you, He loves you, He loves you! His heart is to see you soar and be all you can be.

In the next chapter, we will look at what it means to be immersed in the perfect love of the triune God—Father, Son, and Holy Spirit.

Journey into Perfect Love

We invite you to say this prayer of encounter:

Jesus, as I read the pages of this book, I ask You to help me encounter the fire of Your perfect love and be filled with strength and courage to pursue a life of love.

Recalibrate my heart to love You above all else, to enter the fire of God's burning affections, and to know and experience all the delights of Your heart. I receive grace and comfort to stay in the intensity of Your burning, holy fire that marks and sets me apart. I ask for the fire of God's perfect love to continue to fill me until all fear and anxiety are cast out and all hindrances that keep me from seeing how much You love me are burned up.

Jesus, I want the search for Your face and love to remain at my finish line. I pray that the fire on the altar of my heart will never go out. Amid my struggles and trials, I declare that the fire of perfect love will be my true north and my perfect peace. As I pursue love and make it my goal, I will feast on the abundance of Your love and see more clearly the pathway to my destiny.

An audible version of a prayer to receive the fire of perfect love by us, Steven and Rene, is available on our website www.globalpresence.com/PerfectLove.

TWO

Immersed in the Nature of Triune Love

Go therefore and make disciples of all the nations [help the people to learn of Me, believe in Me, and obey My words], baptizing [immersing] them in the name of the Father and of the Son and of the Holy Spirit.

Matthew 28:19 AMP

Rene

When I was a teenager, a friend was struggling with a bad reputation due to her promiscuity. People judged her without knowing her story. She shared with me that the only way she could feel a sense of being loved was through sex. As a young girl, her father had molested her repeatedly and told her that was how love is expressed. Even though she had been removed from her father, she left with the pain of molestation and a distorted image of love. So, as a teenager, she found herself trying to find love and value in being promiscuous, which left her empty and confused.

Later in life, through the power of God's love, my friend was able to identify the lies she had believed, and she found emotional healing through the pure love of her heavenly Father.

This scenario may not be your story, but your circumstances may also have distorted or misdefined love. Every person on planet earth requires a redefinition of love and an immersion in true, unconditional love.

What is the core nature of God? As we stated in chapter 1, God not only loves, but He *is* love. What does it mean to be immersed in this love? It means letting go of everything that is not love, embracing all that is love, and becoming a completely new creation. Being immersed in the nature of God is to be immersed in the essence of love.

When Jesus told His followers to "go and make disciples of all nations, baptizing them in the name of the Father and of the Son and of the Holy Spirit" (Matthew 28:19 NIV), He was commissioning them to immerse—Greek, *baptizo*, to completely saturate—people and entire nations in the nature, essence, and character of the Triune God. God is the good Father who created us for relationship, the sacrificial Son who redeemed us with His life, and the Holy Spirit, who patiently pursues and transforms us with truth.

To help us understand God's character and the nature of love, let's look at His original intent for humankind and His extravagant expression of love throughout all of Scripture. We will see that everything God does is love because He is love. This is His nature. He cannot help but love. We can also see that the world's definition of love is different from God's.

If we are to let the power of perfect love transform us to be love in the same way that God is love, we must be clear about what love is and where it comes from, so we can represent and *be* that love on the earth.

From the Beginning of Creation

The book of Genesis presents a clear picture of how God expressed His love through creation from the very beginning. Nothing was created accidentally, but purposefully and extravagantly. From what was formless and empty, God created the heavens and earth as a magnificent display of His beauty and splendor.

God's creative power was far more than a "big bang"; it was the majestic sound of love setting the creative order in place. Galaxies spun into existence, time was birthed, and the universe erupted with praise to God as heaven and earth marvelously displayed the beauty and splendor of their Maker.

We see the triune nature of God creating together in perfect harmony: with movement, as the Spirit of God hovered over darkness; with wisdom, as Father God made way for life to come forth from His power, creativity, and love; and with sound, as Jesus Christ gave voice to the Father's desires with each word that proceeded from His mouth.

We also see the Father, Son, and Spirit at work in creating humankind. In Genesis 1:26, God said, "Let us make mankind in our image, in our likeness" (NIV). Here we see the harmonious intimacy of the Triune God in the creation man in "our" (plural!) likeness. Why? Because of love.

Let's dive more deeply into that love by looking more specifically at the role of each Person of the Trinity.

The Perfect Love of a Good Father

As we marvel at the vastness of God's creative power, we are deeply touched by His tender affection in the creation of man and woman. In this intimate moment, God kneels in the soil, and with His hands forms Adam tenderly in His own image. Right from the start we see that God does not mind getting His hands dirty. (More on this in future chapters.)

> Yahweh-God scooped up a lump of soil, sculpted a man, and blew into his nostrils the breath of life. The man came alive—a living soul! Then Yahweh-God planted a lush garden paradise in the East, in the Land of Delight, and there he placed the man he had formed.
>
> Genesis 2:7–8 TPT

Face to face, God breathes life into Adam, awakening him in the perfection of love. The very first image Adam would have looked upon was the face of his Maker. From our very beginning, we were made to behold the glory of God.

Father God was delighted to share with Adam the mere task of—oh, just naming every animal He had created! He was giving Adam the ability to identify and define the world around him. We might imagine that God was right there with him, doing it together.

The Father's Love

God wants us to enjoy the newness of creation in the same way He does, like a proud parent looking at the newborn baby, marveling at whose eyes or ears or toes the baby has, and dreaming of the life they will share together.

God created man and woman and shaped them with his image inside of them. In his own beautiful image, he created his masterpiece.

Genesis 1:27 TPT

God shaped man and woman with His own image inside of them. We are His beautiful masterpiece. He formed the woman from out of the man's side—an equal, someone to complete him, to be next to his heart, to love and cherish. Their relationship with God was the centerpiece from which all other relationships were meant to flow—marriage, children, community. Can you feel the tender care and rich love of God in this process?

God made humans with the choice to respond to Him through love and trust, not fear and control. Father God's intent in creating us is clear in Genesis: He wanted a family to share life with. It was never about control and rules.

Knowing the Father's original intent in creation helps us understand His perfect love and combat accusations against His character. It was not God's intent for us to experience death, suffering, pain, separation, shame, disharmony, hostility, the power struggle between men and women, or toil in our work. All these are the result of the curse brought about by the disobedience (sin) of man.

God's actions in Genesis 1–3 reveal much about His nature and character. Let's take a closer look at the attributes of Father God and the beauty of the intent of His heart.

To Express Love, Father God . . .

- Gives life (Genesis 1)
- Gives authority over creation (Genesis 1:26–28)

- Celebrates His creation (Genesis 1:31)
- Sets apart a day of rest (Genesis 2:3)
- Is intimate (Genesis 2:7)
- Delights (*Eden* in Hebrew is the land of "delight," Genesis 2:8)
- Provides a home with everything needed (Genesis 2:8–9)
- Is abundantly generous (Genesis 2:9)
- Makes things beautiful (Genesis 2:9–14)
- Confers responsibility (Genesis 2:15, 19)
- Protects and gives freedom to choose (Genesis 2:16–17)
- Spends time (Genesis 2:19–20)
- Provides companionship (Genesis 2:18, 21–22)
- Redeems (Genesis 3:15)
- Clothes and covers (Genesis 3:21)
- Protects from living forever in sin (Genesis 3:22–24)

The Perfect Love of the Sacrificial Son

Although the disobedience of Adam and Eve in eating from the forbidden tree resulted in death and separation from God, it did not change His extravagant love and care for them. His action in covering Adam and Eve's shame with animal skin, requiring the shedding of blood, gives us insight into just how far love's perfection will go to cover and restore us. God does not shame us in our faults; He covers us and wraps us in His love.

And He made plans to redeem us. He told the serpent in Genesis 3:15 that Eve's seed or "offspring" (NIV) would crush his head, in a foreshadowing of Jesus, the incorruptible seed, God's one and only Son, who would die in our place to reconcile us to the Father.

The Son's Love

The self-sacrificial love of Jesus does for us what we could not do for ourselves. His atoning death forgives the sins of all who put their faith in Him and restores us to a relationship with our heavenly Father, who declares us righteous. And it gives us authority to release the greater reality of God's Kingdom on earth.

Jesus' powerful act of love echoes throughout eternity and into the recesses of our soul: "It is finished!" (John 19:30 NIV). When we receive the weight of the revelation of God's perfect love being poured out on the cross through Jesus Christ as payment for our sins, it transforms us from the inside out. "God demonstrates His own love for us in this: While we were still sinners, Christ died for us" (Romans 5:8 NIV). Our part is simply to believe, receive, and respond to what God initiated.

What kind of love is this, expressed through Jesus Christ, as His passion for us pursued us all the way from heaven? Jesus actually stepped out of the glorious riches of heaven as *Immanuel* ("God with us"), wrapped Himself in the frailty of humanity, entered our brokenness and pain, lived a sinless life, humbled Himself in obedience to death for our sins, destroyed the power of death and the works of the devil, calls imperfect people to do greater works than He did, and offers us abundant life in Him. Wow!

Envision with me the deep mysteries unveiled of God's perfect love. Paul prays

> that you, being rooted and grounded in love, may be able to comprehend with all the saints what is the <u>width</u> and <u>length</u> and <u>depth</u> and <u>height</u>—to know the love of Christ which passes knowledge; that you may be filled with all the fullness of God.
> Ephesians 3:17–19 (emphasis added)

The *width* of the love of Christ welcomes us with arms spread wide open, once nailed to the cross. He gives an invitation: "This is how much I love you. Will you embrace My love in return and expose your heart to Me?"

The *length* of the love of Christ transcends time and space. From the top of His thorn-pierced head to the bottom of His nail-pierced feet, He loves you with His entire being. Jesus is the bridge to reconcile us to our heavenly Father, to give us full access to the resources of heaven while on earth, and to bring us to eternal life in heaven. Jesus' redeeming eyes of love are looking at you now, inviting you to come into His Father's house, where a banquet table of His love will be set for you to experience the goodness of God.

The *depth* of the love of Christ is stronger than the grave. Jesus' radical obedience to death brought Him to the grave and into the depths of hell to take back the keys—the authority—given over to Satan by Adam's disobedience. His humility was demonstrated in His willingness to lay down His life so we can choose eternal life through Him.

The *height* of the love of Christ is so extravagant that it reaches to the heavens. Jesus rose again on the third day, demonstrating resurrection power, and is now seated at the right hand of our Father in heaven,

> far above all principality and power and might and dominion, and every name that is named, not only in this age but also in that which is to come. And [God] put all things under His feet, and gave Him to be the head over all things to the church.
>
> Ephesians 1:21–22

Extending His hand to you, Christ says, "Beloved, as you go low, you must also rise up into the fullness of My love, grace, and power. Will you take My hand and assume your royal position with Me at the right hand of our Father?"

To Express Love, Jesus . . .

- Is perfect, holy, and righteous (Hebrews 5:9; 1 Peter 1:15; 1 John 2:1)
- Is full of grace and truth (John 1:14)
- Is humble and obedient (Philippians 2:5–8)
- Saves (Luke 19:10; John 3:16–17)
- Atones for our sins (Hebrews 2:17)
- Destroys the power of death and the devil's works (Hebrews 2:14–15; 1 John 3:8)
- Is victorious over sin (1 Corinthians 15:55–57)
- Brings reconciliation (Romans 5:10–11; 2 Corinthians 5:18–19)
- Brings peace (Ephesians 2:14–17)
- Sacrifices (John 15:13; Hebrews 9:26)
- Forgives with no record of wrong (1 Corinthians 13:5)
- Speaks truth (John 8:31–32; 14:6)
- Welcomes (Romans 15:7)
- Casts out fear (1 John 4:18)
- Heals (Matthew 9:35; 12:15)
- Binds up the brokenhearted (Isaiah 61:1; Luke 4:18)
- Delivers, sets captives free (Luke 4:18; Acts 10:38)
- Brings the Good News (Isaiah 61:1–2; Luke 4:18-19)
- Restores (Matthew 12:13)
- Gives abundant life (John 10:10)

- Confronts sin (John 8:33–34), Satan (Matthew 4:1–11), hypocritical leaders (Matthew 23:13–36)
- Bears burdens (Matthew 11:28–30; 1 Peter 5:7)
- Expresses compassion (Matthew 14:14; 20:34)
- Serves (Mark 10:45; John 13:14)
- Satisfies thirst (John 4:13–14)
- Intercedes for us (Romans 8:34)
- Yields to the Father (John 6:38)
- Brings light to darkness (John 12:46)

The Perfect Love of Holy Spirit

What a beautiful gift we have been given from the Father in the promised Holy Spirit! We love the way the apostle Paul describes Him in Ephesians 1:14 (TPT):

> He is given to us like an engagement ring, as the first installment of what's coming! He is our hope-promise of a future inheritance which seals us until we have all of redemption's promises and experience complete freedom—all for the supreme glory and honor of God!

Holy Spirit infused Jesus' life on earth. Jesus was conceived by the Spirit. At His baptism, the Spirit descended on Him visibly. Holy Spirit led Jesus into the wilderness and brought Him out in power. Jesus' first public sermon began with the words "The Spirit of the LORD is upon Me" (Luke 4:18). Jesus healed and cast out demons by the power of the Spirit. And as a final crescendo, Holy Spirit raised Jesus from the dead (see Romans 8:11). If Jesus needed the power of Holy Spirit, how much more do we?

Jesus knew this when He instructed His disciples to wait for the promised Holy Spirit to come upon them to receive power. The 120 in the Upper Room were given what they needed—power, courage, and fresh fire.

The Spirit's Love

To experience the fire of perfect love, we must recognize and yield to the work of God's Spirit. Relating to Holy Spirit allows us to live vibrant, passionate lives full of love, grace, and power.

To Express Love, Holy Spirit . . .

- Seals, guarantees salvation (2 Corinthians 1:22; Ephesians 1:13–14)
- Gives life (John 6:63)
- Helps (John 14:16)
- Points to Jesus (John 15:26)
- Gives grace and supplication (Zechariah 12:10; Hebrews 10:29)
- Guides into all truth (John 14:17; 16:13)
- Brings comfort (Acts 9:31)
- Brings freedom (2 Corinthians 3:17)
- Convicts and empowers (John 16:8; Romans 8:13)
- Brings oneness (1 Corinthians 12:13)
- Brings adoption (Romans 8:15–16)
- Gives access to the Father (Ephesians 2:18)
- Brings wind and fire (Acts 2:2–3)
- Gives power and boldness (Acts 1:8; 4:31)

- Sanctifies and transforms (Romans 15:16; 1 Corinthians 6:11; 2 Corinthians 3:18)
- Leads (Luke 4:1; Romans 8:14)
- Anoints (Luke 4:18)
- Fills (Ephesians 5:18)
- Clothes and strengthens with power (Luke 24:49; Ephesians 3:16)
- Gives wisdom, understanding, counsel, might, knowledge, fear of the Lord (Isaiah 11:2)
- Gives revelation (Ephesians 1:17)
- Teaches (1 Corinthians 2:13)
- Gives discernment (1 Corinthians 2:14)
- Gives spiritual gifts (1 Corinthians 12:4, 7–11)
- Intercedes for us (Romans 8:26–27)
- Helps us pray (Ephesians 6:18)
- Gives righteousness, peace, joy (Acts 13:52; Romans 14:17)
- Works holiness in us (1 Thessalonians 4:7–8)
- Circumcises our hearts (Romans 2:29)
- Empowers us as witnesses (Acts 1:8)

Journey into Perfect Love

By looking at the nature of the Triune God, we hope you have seen that God expresses extravagant love toward you all the time. He cannot help but love because He is love, and we must define love through His nature alone.

48

Now that you have been saturated in the way each Person of the Trinity expresses love toward you, may the perfect love of the Triune God wash over you as you receive His words of deep affection.

I am the God who created you and called you by name.

My very breath is the life within you. My child, you are an original design, My masterpiece. I cherish you and am always with you. You can trust Me with your whole heart.

I planned from the foundation of the world to redeem you to Myself. My love for you reaches higher than the heavens. Even the depths of the grave could not hold back My love for you. My heart and arms are wide open to you. You have full access to My heart and to the throne of grace. Allow My face to become your great joy. I am the strength that upholds you.

I have sealed you with the fire of My perfect love. I will continue to lead you into all truth. Allow the fire of My perfect love to awaken you to the fullness of My love in you.

For more of God's perfect love audibly spoken over you accompanied by the prophetic sounds of heaven, please see our IMMERSE soaking series available on our website www.global presence.com/PerfectLove.

THREE

The Sound of Awakening

"And the angel who was speaking with me came back and awakened me, like a man who is awakened out of his sleep."

Zechariah 4:1 AMP

For generations the enemy has been releasing a lullaby spirit into the atmosphere. But God has the answer in this day and hour that will cause many hearts to wake from sleep and burn with His fiery passion and love. It is the sound of awakening.

Some of us are being awakened to the sweet, tender whispers of the Father. Some of us are being awakened to the passion of the Bridegroom. And some of us are being awakened to the power and grace that come from the Spirit of truth, Holy Spirit.

God is releasing the sound of awakening, with all of heaven behind Him. All will hear but not all will respond.

The Angels of Awakening

Steven

Recently I have had four different encounters with angels of awakening. Each encounter released a fresh dimension of awakening into the spiritual atmosphere.

During the fourth encounter, I saw four large angels who came from the four corners of the earth. They were holding gongs, like cymbals, that they would strike. Every time they struck a gong, it would reverberate and release seismic waves of love in every direction from the heart of the Father. I realized these were the sounds of awakening being released.

Behind each of the four angels with the gongs was a set of two more angels—eight in all—with large, shiny shofars like trumpets. As the resonance of the gongs was releasing seismic waves of love, these eight angels began to blow their trumpets. I knew they were calling the Bride to attention. The *dut da dut da dut* blast of the trumpets was awakening the spirits of God's people.

Behind each set of trumpeters was a set of five more angels—twenty in all—holding large sickles. When I first saw them, they were sharpening the edges of their sickles against a sharpening stone. The Lord began to whisper: "The reason for this is that hearts will be awakened to My love and burning passion for them. This is the sound of the Spirit, who calls My people to attention—attention to Me and attention to the harvest."

All at once, the harvest angels were ready. The Lord said to me, "Speak to them now and release them to the winds of My Spirit in all directions." So I spoke and released them: "Angels of awakening, be released to the north!" Immediately those angels were released to the north. Then the Lord said, "Release My angels to the south!" and I released the angels to the south. Then He said, "Release the angels to the east!" and they were released to the east. "Release My angels to the west!" and they were released to the west.

As each of the angels disappeared, riding the wind of the Spirit in each direction, I thought, *We are in for a historic move of God as this awakening is at hand.*

The Call to Awakening

Angels of awakening are beginning to be released on the four winds of the Spirit that will lead to the great end-time harvest. We read about this awakening in Scripture:

"The angel who was speaking with me came back and awakened me, like a man who is awakened out of his sleep" (Zechariah 4:1 AMP).

"He will send His angels with a great sound of a trumpet, and they will gather together His elect from the four winds, from one end of heaven to the other" (Matthew 24:31).

We also read about awakening in Isaiah:

"Arise, shine; for your light has come, and the glory of the LORD has risen upon you. For behold, darkness will cover the earth and deep darkness the peoples; but the LORD will rise upon you and His glory will appear upon you. Nations will come to your light, and kings to the brightness of your rising."

Isaiah 60:1–3 NASB

The Church has been asleep for a long time. But no more! We are being called to wake up. Those with ears to hear will hear what the Spirit is saying, just as Jesus said to the seven churches in Revelation 2–3. Although not everyone has an ear to hear, those who do will receive the reality that we are called to arise.

Too often we in the Church have focused on the darkness, the grim, the gloom, but God is calling us to a higher place—that we would arise and shine, clothed in His glory. "Nations will come to [our] light" as we shine in the midst of darkness. We will even be called to stand before kings and CEOs and influencers on the planet, who will come "to the brightness of [our] rising." Kings in the midst of darkness are longing to hear what God is saying, and we have the radiance and hope of glory inside of us.

It is your turn to shine. So shine!

Revelation and Unveiling

Awakening is brought about by revelation and unveiling, when we see Jesus as He really is:

> I pray that the Father of glory, the God of our Lord Jesus Christ, would impart to you the riches of the Spirit of wisdom and the Spirit of revelation to know him through your deepening intimacy with him. I pray that the light of God will illuminate the eyes of your imagination, flooding you with light, until you experience the full revelation of the hope of his calling—that is, the wealth of God's glorious inheritances that he finds in us, his holy ones!
>
> Ephesians 1:17–18 TPT

In the midst of God's glory, there is an unveiling. Jesus wants you to know Him more deeply and intimately. This is the beauty of the awakening fire that brings "the full revelation of the hope of his calling," so you can become all God has called you to be.

We encourage you to declare this prayer over your life, from the very depths of your being. Discovery will be released as you believe and declare "that the Father of glory" will give you "the Spirit of wisdom and the Spirit of revelation."

In the wisdom dimension, we gain keen insight and understanding. In the revelation dimension, we gain understanding of what the enemy has put into place and the reality of the season in which we live. This is what the sons of Issachar operated in, who "understood the times and knew what Israel should do" (1 Chronicles 12:32 NIV).

As the Church awakens, we will see Jesus as He is and the fullness of our inheritance in Him. He really is the King of Glory. He is the Lover of our souls. There is no one like Him.

Do you remember the childhood story of Sleeping Beauty? The Church is the beauty in the story, but she has been asleep to the greater purpose and abundant life Jesus promised her. In the story, the only thing that can break the curse is the kiss of the prince. In our case it is the kiss of the King's Word and His love that bring the awakening that leads to reformation. We are entering a season when God is going to kiss us with the treasures and goodness of His Word. He longs for His Bride to arise in bold, confident love.

Invitation from the Bridegroom

In Song of Songs 2:10, we are called to arise and come away with our Beloved. The word *arise* in Hebrew comes from the word *qum*, reflecting when the Levites took up the Ark of the Covenant, carrying the glory on their shoulders as they moved the Ark through the wilderness. The word *arise* in Hebrew also means "to abide, to establish, to stir up, to strengthen, to succeed." As we are kings and priests to our God, according to Revelation 1:6, we, too, carry God's presence wherever we go.

So Jesus invites us to come away with Him, to be drawn into a new dimension of His heart and goodness toward us.

In Song of Songs 2:12 (TPT), the Bridegroom King says:

> The season for singing and pruning the vines has arrived. I hear the cooing of doves in our land, filling the air with songs to awaken you and guide you forth.

The season of change is upon us—a season like none that has ever been seen before, even in the early centuries of the Church. This season will bring about a new song and a time for "pruning the vines," when God begins to remove the good things to make room for the great things.

The sound of "the cooing of doves" speaks to a fresh dimension of peace. In this cold, dark season, the sound of *shalom* is being released and filling the air with songs.

Verse 14 (TPT) continues:

> For you are my dove, hidden in the split-open rock. It was I who took you and hid you up high in the secret stairway of the sky. Let me see your radiant face and hear your sweet voice. How beautiful your eyes of worship and lovely your voice in prayer.

God is inviting us into a deeper and higher place. The Passion Translation calls it "the secret stairway of the sky." As we encounter His intimacy through the sweetness of His Word, the uncreated God is saying, "I want to see your face because it's lovely. I want to hear your voice because it awakens My heart. It brings pleasure to me. It's delightful." Can you imagine that? He wants to see your eyes. He wants to hear your voice. He wants your complete being to be engaged with Him.

It is not that God needs anything, but when we hold back our hearts and our worship from Him, there is actually a void in God's heart. He created us for relationship, and these intimate encounters bring an elation of love from the heart of God that overwhelms us. What else can we do but give that love back to Him?

> Who is this one? She arises out of her desert, clinging to her beloved. When I awakened you under the apple tree, as you were feasting upon me, I awakened your innermost being with the travail of birth as you longed for more of me.
>
> Song of Songs 8:5 TPT

As we hear the tender whispers of the Lord, as we fine-tune our hearts to hear His heart, He deposits in our innermost being what resides in His own heart. Then we become ones who carry the desires of His heart to be born in the earth realm. He could have accomplished all His work with a snap of a finger, but He chose to have a Bride who would be consumed by His glory and grace, to give birth to the desires of His heart in the earth. Everything He does, He does for relationship.

The Bridegroom King gives this invitation: "Fasten me upon your heart as a seal of fire forevermore" (Song of Songs 8:6 TPT). God is a living and consuming fire, sealing and marking a generation with love.

A seal was made by a king in years gone by who would write an edict or decree on a scroll, place a drop of wax on it, and then take his signet ring to mark it. In the same way, the King of kings is sealing a generation with His amazing, fiery love and marking it forevermore. Jesus, the Bridegroom, is saying, "You have been on this journey with Me, but there's a dimension you haven't entered yet. Fasten me as a seal of fire upon your heart forevermore. The living, consuming flame will seal you as a lover, encapsulated in My love. My passion is stronger than the chains of death and the grave. All-consuming are the flashes of fire from My burning heart of love."

Rivers of pain and persecution will never extinguish this flame. Endless floods will be unable to quench this raging fire that burns within you. Everything will be consumed. It will stop at nothing as you yield everything to this furious fire until it won't even seem to you like a sacrifice anymore.

Song of Songs 8:7 TPT

Once this fire is stoked, it cannot be put out. No past, present, or future troubles can extinguish it. This fire will stop at nothing, consuming everything that hinders love.

The Banqueting Table

God is raising a generation after His heart, hungry for the more of all He has for us—more of His presence, more of His pleasure, more of His tender whispers, more of spending time in His presence, more of even spending time with a tribe of people who are also after God's heart.

David, the shepherd king, wrote about walking "through the valley of the shadow of death" (Psalm 23:4) and fearing no evil. David knew God was with him in his shadowy, dark season, and he wrote, "You prepare a table before me in the presence of my enemies" (verse 5).

God brings us to a banqueting table with an incredible feast where we can enjoy all the delicacies of the Kingdom in the presence of our enemies, right when the noise and clamor are the loudest. We just need to change our perspective and see the feast that has been laid out for us.

God wants us not only to feast *with* Him, but to feast *on* Him and on His presence. The Bridegroom says in Song of Songs 8:5, "When I awakened you under the apple tree, as you were feasting upon me . . ." (TPT). You can have as much of God as you want. You can fall into a false humility in which you think you are a burden—when the reality is, God loves to hear your voice and the things that are going on in your heart. He loves being part of your journey.

When your spirit is awakened and your soul says, "I've got to have more of God," then your flesh no longer craves the lesser things, because you have been awakened to the better things. This is part of the pruning we saw in Song of Songs 2:12. You have been awakened not to earthly pleasures, but to the heavenly realm—the banqueting table of His presence where you can feast on the reality of His goodness. "Oh, taste and see that the LORD is good; blessed is the man who trusts in Him!" (Psalm 34:8). Jesus says,

"Blessed [joyful, nourished by God's goodness] are those who hunger and thirst for righteousness [those who actively seek right standing with God], for they will be [completely] satisfied."

Matthew 5:6 AMP

As you hunger and thirst for righteousness, you will be satisfied. And as you are satisfied, your capacity will increase for more of God's presence. Once you have tasted His love and goodness, you have to have more! Moses met with Him daily. David made it a lifestyle to behold His beauty. Jesus met early in the morning with His Father.

Hunger does something powerful. When you are alone with the Lord and your hunger is awakened, it pulls on heaven, attracting the beautiful, fiery love of the Father; it draws that love as through a pipeline, coming right from the heavenly places.

So wake up in a deeper way to the revelation of who God is. Choose to enter intimate encounters with His Word. These provide the feast the Lord has laid out for you, bringing awakening inside your being, so you can be part of the hope being released in the planet for such a time as this.

Jesus is the remedy. If you have put your trust in Him as Savior, you get to be a light bringing transformation and the reality of awakening to the lovers of Jesus and those who will become lovers in the days to come.

Journey into Perfect Love

We invite you to say this prayer of declaration:

Awaken me to the fire of perfect love, taking me into the deeper things of the Spirit, overflowing with Your glory and grace. I declare that my eyes have been unveiled to encounter my deepening intimacy with the King of the universe. I declare that I am flooded with the love and life of Jesus, as I am awakened to the kisses of Your sweet Word. I declare that I am awakened to the feast of Your loving presence, and my hunger will propel me to the delicacies of Your Kingdom and to Your great love.

FOUR

The Exchange of Extravagant Love

Look with wonder at the depth of the Father's marvelous love that he has lavished on us!

1 John 3:1 TPT

"Mary has discovered the one thing most important by choosing to sit at my feet. She is undistracted, and I won't take this privilege from her."

Luke 10:42 TPT

Can you imagine having Jesus as a friend as He walked here on earth? To sit with Him, eat with Him, be taught by Him, and to reason with Him? Imagine Jesus placing His hands on your shoulders or touching your face gently and looking into your eyes. Your eyes locking with His fiery eyes of love and compassion would bring peace to the depths of your soul.

What was it like to feast with Jesus and on every word that proceeded from His mouth? What was it like to sit at His feet or lean on His chest, hearing the rhythm of love in His heart? Only a few individuals were able to experience this in-the-flesh friendship—a friendship that demanded a response.

We will explore this friendship and intimacy, which are still available for us today as the eyes of our hearts are enlightened to see Him. When we respond to what Jesus did for us—atoning for our sins on the cross, setting us free, and giving us an abundant life—it changes everything. When we learn to respond to His love rather than reacting to the appetites of our flesh, in our old nature and old ways of thinking, or according to circumstances, we cultivate friendship and intimacy with the Lord that will awaken fire and passion inside of us.

Our desire to be close to Jesus can be frustrating because we just do not know how to get there, and we can experience blocks in connecting with Him. But by positioning our hearts and allowing His grace to recalibrate our lives, we can sit at the table with Him and feast on His goodness and extravagant love. Learning to receive and respond to what God has initiated takes out the striving—trying to measure up in order to be accepted. Rather, the revelation of God's fiery love for us helps us respond with our own wholehearted love. First John 4:19 says "We love Him because He first loved us." So we receive and respond to what God already initiated.

If you find you are not passionate for God, you may not have come yet into the full revelation of just how passionate He is for you. When you get the revelation of how Jesus gave everything for you, how He poured His life out on the cross, your only reasonable response is to give your whole life to Him and pour out your own love and affection.

Encountering Jesus

When Jesus was making His way to Jerusalem, He often stopped in Bethany along the way. There was something special about this place called Bethany. It is where three of His friends lived, and where Jesus found retreat, relaxation, and refreshment. Yes, the disciples were also His friends, but there was something unique and special in His friendship with Mary, Martha, and Lazarus. Jesus loved to come and hang out with them. Those times were not so much about ministry, as we might think of it, but simply being in the presence of His friends.

God likes to be in the presence of His friends. He likes to be in your presence. If you have said *yes* to Christ and He is your Lord and Savior, He likes to be in your presence. Even if you have not yet said *yes* to Jesus, you are created in His image and He likes to be in your presence. He loves you more than you can imagine.

With our ministry, Global Presence, we often take teams to the nations. On one of our trips to Israel, we met a young woman from Bethany who shared with us her story.

Badaya had been diagnosed with cancer and had only a short time to live. Her mom, brother, and some other family members were Christians, but she was a Muslim who hated both Jewish people and Christians, and wanted nothing to do with their God. She was suffering physically, which filled her with anger and bitterness, making her doubt if there even was a God at all.

So Badaya decided to connect with Hamas, the militant Islamic organization, thinking that the best way to end her life would be a suicide bombing, with her main target as Jewish people. A plan started coming together to bring as much destruction as possible.

At the same time, Badaya's mom kept asking if she could pray with her. She refused. She did not want her mother's prayers. Why would she? She did not even believe this God existed.

The night before she was to carry out the bombing, with nothing to lose, Badaya made a simple decision: *I'm not going to pray to Allah. I'm not going to pray to Jesus. But I'm going to pray to the God who created me, because He can heal me.*

That night while she was sleeping, a Man in white appeared to her and revealed Himself as Jesus, the One who had created her. He placed His hand on her heart. When she woke up the next morning, she knew she was completely healed, and her heart was set free.

From that point on, Badaya began to worship Jesus. The hatred she had had for the Jewish people and Christians was removed in a moment because of her encounter with the Man who had created her for friendship and relationship. She was compelled by that reality to love.

We have heard astounding testimonies firsthand about the Man in white showing Himself to Muslims. God is drawing people to Himself in this day and hour.

The name *Bethany*—the village where Badaya is from, and where Jesus' friends Mary, Martha, and Lazarus lived—has several different meanings. It can mean "the house of affliction," "the house of bitterness," or "the house of song." In the middle of Badaya's affliction, God reached down, touched her through a dream or vision, and brought healing to her, so that she would sing the song of God's extravagant love. He is alive today, and right now He is looking for friends.

Steven

Two years later we were in Jerusalem, along with our daughter, Elizabeth, almost eleven, visiting a wonderful house of prayer overlooking Mount Zion. In the weekly equipping service that evening, a young man came in, dragging his leg. As he crossed the room, I thought, *God is going to heal that man.* And as I was preaching the message, I told him three different times, "God is going to heal you," even though I had no idea what was wrong with him.

Later, as Rene and our team offered prophetic and healing prayer for anyone who needed it, I called the man forward. A believer in the Messiah, he told Elizabeth and me that one of his hamstring tendons had been severed, so there was no way he could bend his leg. I could feel the muscle rolled up under the skin on the back of his leg. He was supposed to go in for surgery that week.

Elizabeth and I began to pray for him, releasing healing into him. Suddenly he felt the fire of God's healing power. My hands were on his leg. The balled-up muscle was gone; the tendon had reattached, and he could now bend his leg. He jumped up and started to run around the room, praising Jesus excitedly.

"Wow!" he exclaimed. "The doctors aren't going to believe this!"

"You know who to give credit to," I replied. "Jesus, the Messiah!"

"Yes, I'll tell them Jesus healed me!"

As it turns out, this man was the brother of Badaya, the woman from Bethany who had been healed by Jesus in her vision. Both had encountered the extravagant love of God poured out.

Making Jesus First

The Bible tells about one of the times Jesus and His disciples visited Bethany and stopped at the home of His friends Mary,

Martha, and Lazarus. Martha got busy in the kitchen preparing the meal and getting everything ready for their honored guest and His disciples. Not Mary.

> Mary sat down attentively before the Master, absorbing every revelation he shared. But Martha became exasperated with finishing the numerous household chores in preparation for her guests, so she interrupted Jesus and said, "Lord, don't you think it's unfair that my sister left me to do all the work by myself? You should tell her to get up and help me."
>
> Luke 10:39–40 TPT

Martha was exasperated and complaining, while Mary sat at Jesus' feet, gazing at Him and listening intently to every word. She was drawn into His heart, her own heart being awakened and made alive.

> The Lord answered her, "Martha, my beloved Martha. Why are you upset and troubled, pulled away by all these many distractions? Mary has discovered the one thing most important by choosing to sit at my feet. She is undistracted, and I won't take this privilege from her."
>
> verses 41–42 TPT

The issue Jesus was addressing was not the fact that she was serving, but the way she was going about it. He noted that she was upset, troubled and distracted. Was she trying to prove her love and affection by what she was doing? Many of us are like that. God loves people who serve, who do things. The doers are the ones who get things done. But if we strive after the "doing" first, all we do is "do, do, do." Instead God is calling us to *do* from a place of *being*.

From the place of being at the feet of Jesus, we are in a better position to hear and respond to what He has called us to do.

There are all kinds of things that must be done. For example, Jesus exhorted us to "pray the Lord of the harvest to send out laborers into His harvest" (Luke 10:2). Labor means you are doing something. That is work. And James said that "faith without works is dead" (James 2:20). But works must come out of a heart fascinated with the beauty of Jesus Christ. This awakens the reality of who lives inside of us—"Christ in you, the hope of glory" (Colossians 1:27).

There is something God wants to awaken in your heart today so you really see what is on the inside—and it is He Himself! He is jealous for you. He is jealous for your affection. He is jealous for your time. You may feel you do not have the time, but you are called to worship Him in all things. You can worship while you work, while you drive—even, if you are a student, in your homework. It is amazing that when you give God just that morsel of your attention, He causes everything to fall in line. When you make Him the priority, He really does become first in your life.

Extravagant Love

Sometime later we see that things changed with Martha:

> Six days before the Passover began, Jesus went back to Bethany, the town where he raised Lazarus from the dead. They had prepared a supper for Jesus. Martha served, and Lazarus and Mary were among those at the table.
>
> John 12:1–2 TPT

In this instance, we do not see Jesus rebuking Martha, but embracing her through her worship as she served. No longer worried and striving, Martha was now serving while understanding who He was. She had spent time with Him. She had come to realize that her sister *had* chosen the better thing.

Her response to Jesus in that earlier encounter was probably not irritation or a dismissive "Yeah, whatever." She had taken it to heart and begun to practice His presence. She had begun to sit at Jesus' feet in the same way Mary did. She learned to *do* from a place of being with Jesus. Her doing was now an expression of her worship. And she had come to know and trust Him far more deeply after He raised her brother from the dead.

When we look at Lazarus sitting at the table with Jesus—Lazarus who was dead not long ago!—that is pretty crazy. His literal presence was a witness testifying of God's amazing power and grace.

Witnessing is not always about saying things. Lazarus was not witnessing at all; he was being a witness. In Acts 1:8, Jesus said:

> "You shall receive power when the Holy Spirit has come upon you; and you shall be witnesses to Me in Jerusalem, and in all Judea and Samaria, and to the end of the earth."

He did not say they would *go* witness; they would *be* witnesses, because they would be empowered by Holy Spirit. Because of Jesus' love poured out, they would in turn pour out His Spirit to others. Being a witness is a reality of identity. God is looking for witnesses. Lazarus sitting at that table, and the fact that he had been dead and was now alive again spoke volumes.

Something else spoke volumes to those at the table, and to every Christian in the two thousand years since then:

> Mary picked up an alabaster jar filled with nearly a liter of extremely rare and costly perfume—the purest extract of nard,

and she anointed Jesus' feet. Then she wiped them dry with her long hair. And the fragrance of the costly oil filled the house.

John 12:3 TPT

Mary of Bethany loved sitting at the feet of Jesus, and she wanted to give everything to Him because she saw His matchless worth. Even when the disciples did not get it, Mary understood and saw what others did not see. So she came to the table holding an alabaster box containing a pound of anointing oil. Some commentaries say that this oil was likely her dowry—the very thing she was to give to her future husband—because it was worth a year's wages (John 12:5 NIV). But Mary had counted the cost. She broke the alabaster box, part of her inheritance, and anointed the feet of Jesus.

It was a place of worship, giving her all, and she poured it out, and poured it out, and poured it out.

As Mary anointed His feet and dried them with her hair, she may have seen something in the realm of the Spirit that Jesus was about to go on a journey that no other human being had taken—the journey that would bring all of humanity to the place where we could say "yes and amen" to living forever. The Father may have shared secrets with Mary, in that place of sitting at Jesus' feet, because she was a friend of God.

Jesus had told His disciples several times that He would be delivered into the hands of sinners, be killed, and then raised to life (see, for example, Mark 9:31), but they had not really heard it. But Mary may have seen or sensed what would take place just a few days from then, when Jesus would be humiliated, beaten, bruised, and hung on a cross, unrecognizable, to die; and now she poured out her love on her Savior.

But Judas the locksmith, Simon's son, the betrayer, spoke up and said, "What a waste! We could have sold this perfume for a fortune and given the money to the poor!"

(In fact, Judas had no heart for the poor. He only said this because he was a thief and in charge of the money case. He would steal money whenever he wanted from the funds given to support Jesus' ministry.)

Jesus said to Judas, "Leave her alone! She has saved it for the time of my burial. You'll always have the poor with you; but you won't always have me."

John 12:4–8 TPT

Judas Iscariot's name means "Judas the locksmith." It was apparently the trade of his family. Judas was a businessman. John's gospel says he was actually a thief who would pull out and take the money he wanted. Judas held the keys to the money box, but Jesus held the keys to the Kingdom, keys to abundant life. Judas knew the worth of the anointing oil but not the worth of the Man sitting with him at the table.

Mary, on the other hand, saw and beheld the lavish love that would never fail, never fade. She and her sister were compelled to worship because they had encountered Love. Love is not a feeling or emotion. Love is a Person—the Man Christ Jesus. Mary was enthralled by the beauty of who He is, and He was enthralled by her act of worship as she poured out her life and inheritance on Him.

Worship Poured Out

First John 3:1 says, "See what great love the Father has lavished on us, that we should be called children of God" (NIV). The verb *lavish* means "to expend or give in great amounts or without limit; extravagantly, abundantly, or wastefully." God in

His kindness and goodness poured out His love without limit—extravagantly, wastefully. It was not a waste to Him; it was a joy.

The world asks, "Why spend time in a prayer room or go to church on Sunday? There are so many other things to do—like watch football. Relax after working all week. Get out to the mall." And on and on. Why the waste? But when we make Jesus the goal and the priority, and when we bring that priority into our lives—being fascinated with His beauty, His glory, and His grace—everything else comes into alignment.

God is awakening the hearts of sons and daughters in this hour who are willing, like Mary of Bethany, to pour their love out to Him in extravagant measure.

He is asking you today: Are you willing to pour out your love and give it away? Do you want to know the things that are deep in the heart of God? God is looking for worshipers:

> The hour is coming and now is, when the true worshipers will worship the Father in spirit and truth; for the Father is seeking such to worship Him. God is Spirit, and those who worship Him must worship in spirit and truth.
>
> John 4:23–24

Being a worshiper does not mean someone who plays an instrument. Being a worshiper is what God has called each of us to do who has said yes to Jesus. Jesus is looking for the yes and the want-to. Do you want to love Him with all your heart and soul and strength and mind? Worship is a lifestyle. It is about taking baby steps toward that lifestyle. Each day as we take those steps toward Him, we draw a little closer to His heart of love.

So carve out time in your schedule and just begin to worship. Also, when you are walking, take out the earbuds and listen for the voice of the Father. When you are driving, turn off the radio and listen for the voice of the Father. He is always speaking. We need to be listening.

You *can* hear the voice of God. Everyone who has received Jesus as Lord and Savior has heard the voice of God. It is His voice and kindness that brought you to where you could understand how much you needed Him and how much He loves you.

Baby steps were Martha's journey. She was busy, busy, busy. But when Jesus said that Mary had chosen the better way, Martha apparently decided to try it and found it to be good. So the next time Jesus had dinner with His friends from Bethany, Martha's serving came not from what she did, but from knowing who she was as a lover of Jesus.

Too often we draw our identity from the things we do rather than who we are. The fact is, we have all been created in God's image, to be His friends, to be lovers of the Most High God.

When you are willing to lay down your life in extravagant worship, people might call you a Jesus freak. Good! We, Steven and Rene, are Jesus freaks and good with it. King David was a freak, too. His knowledge of God's presence and experience of worship started when he was a boy in the fields, looking after his father's sheep. It became part of the rhythm of his life.

So be a Jesus freak, and you will be fruitful.

What is He worth to you? Are you willing to give Him five minutes a day, or five minutes more? Are you willing to give Him an hour or more? He loves you, and there is nothing you can do to get Him to love you more. Even as Mary poured the oil onto Jesus' feet, He already loved her deeply. The dimension and depth of His love for her did not change—but it awakened something in her.

An entire generation is coming that will be like Mary and David. They will not care what people think; they will just be extravagant in the way they pour their lives out before the King. It will look different for every one of us, but this is what we were created for and what God wants each of us to do—to pour out our songs, our poems, our struggles, our lives to Him.

As you do, something amazing will happen. You will actually minister to the heart of God and become a fragrant offering to him. You will begin to hear His love songs over you, and then sing love songs back to him. When your life is "a living sacrifice, holy and pleasing to God" (Romans 12:1 NIV), this moves His heart.

You are alive in this specific window of time. You have been set apart for this time and marked to do great things. But it is from the place of worship and extravagant love that He will carry you along. From the place of extravagant worship, you will serve God in a way that you have never known before. From the place of extravagant worship, you will continue pouring it out. And from the place of extravagant worship, you will be His witness.

It takes oil for a flame to burn in a lampstand. God is looking for burning hearts. He is raising up a generation so compelled by the first commandment to love Him completely, with all they are, that they can effectively obey the second commandment, which is serving and loving the community around them.

So before you minister to others, receive from God and minister back to Him. That is your first ministry. Pouring out your love is the outflow and byproduct of spending time in His presence and taking time to see Him as He really is—to see that He really is good and that He has good things planned for you.

Journey into Perfect Love

Ask yourself the following questions and see what Holy Spirit shows you:

- What area of my life is most in need of God's extravagant love?
- Where have I received the extravagant love of God in the past, and how can I posture myself to receive His extravagant love in an area of need?
- What are different ways I enjoy pouring out my extravagant worship upon Jesus? What is a new way I can explore pouring out my love upon Him?

Lord, thank You for calling me friend and inviting me to sit at Your feet. I ask for the grace to receive Your extravagant, matchless love. As I encounter Your perfect love, I will be forever changed. Help me not be distracted by the lesser things in life. I pray that as I break open the oil of my life on Your feet, Jesus, that my extravagant life of worship will bring You joy and pleasure, and that it will fill the world around me with the fragrance of Christ.

For God's extravagant love spoken over you, accompanied by the prophetic music, see our complete IMMERSE soaking series available on our website www.globalpresence.com/PerfectLove.

FIVE

Identity Revealed in Perfect Love

Look with wonder at the depth of the Father's marvelous love that he has lavished on us! He has called us and made us his very own beloved children. . . .

1 John 3:1 TPT

Steven

One of my greatest joys is our work in the Republic of Ghana, West Africa, where we opened a home for orphaned and at-risk children (Hope Home) and a private Christian elementary school (Hope Academy) to bless children with the goodness and love of God. Our base is called the Global Presence Transformation Center.

When we first began our work in Ghana and walked through the local villages, my heart was struck by the deep, systemic poverty that plagues the land. There is great need for good nutrition, clean water, daily resources, education, and most of all the knowledge of Father God's unfailing love—the love that sets captives free and unveils the truth that we are destined to be adopted into the family of God. Great joy is often birthed from places of great sorrow.

One day while I was praying at the Transformation Center, I could hear children singing and the rhythm of African drums in the distance. I began to ponder how great the Lord's love is. I was overwhelmed and my heart was bursting with gladness, hearing those sweet children worship the one true God with all their hearts. The thought crossed my mind: *We get to be part of changing the world with God's love.*

As the drums continued, I was taken into an encounter with the Father, and I began to hear the rhythm of our heavenly Father's heartbeat. It was a steady pulse of love being released in all directions. I began to see His love overtaking the darkness and poverty in the land, and royal sons and daughters rising up in victory and freedom. As the heartbeat got louder and more intense, I could feel the vibrations of His love for the people. His heartbeat echoed in every fiber of my being until His sound became my sound. God encountered me with the vibrations of His love so that, through me, others also could experience His sound of love.

The Father longs for you, too, to encounter the vibrations of His love today. Be prepared in this chapter to encounter the rhythm of His perfect love that unveils who you really are: a royal child of the Most High God. As you discover who God has made you to be, you will echo the Father's love to the world around you.

The Importance of Identity

Every human heart longs for a sense of belonging, to be connected with his or her identity and purpose. Until each person discovers this in a relationship with God, many competing substitutes—labels, titles, and causes—try to fill the void. But God longs for beloved sons and daughters to know the truth of their original design—who they are in the core of their being, according to their heavenly, supernatural DNA. We were made by God, who is love, to be perfectly loved and to live out love in a profound way that changes the world.

We live in a generation that has been fascinated by the supernatural, which is why there is a draw to superheroes, fairy-tales, and the concept of moving in and out of realms. But these things are only imitations of what we were created for—moving in and out of heavenly realms, which are even more fulfilling and immersive than these alternatives. After all, the Word of God makes clear that we are not of this world, just strangers passing through. We are to assume the position we are given in Christ, seated with Him in heavenly places, and we receive power to demonstrate the reality of the Kingdom of heaven on earth. We are destined to be the beauties in the fairy story, the valiant warriors, the chosen ones to combat the spiritual forces of evil with the most powerful force in the universe: love!

It is important that we understand that how God sees us—and is at work in us—is from the inside out, from a state of *being* and *relating*. We saw in the last chapter that Martha learned to *do* from a place of *being* with Jesus. Then her doing became an expression of worship. Religion is trying to win God's approval through outward works, while relationship is an inward connection. We are human beings, not human "doings," and God looks past the externals to the heart. Jesus saw in the disciples what others did not see and what the disciples did not see in themselves. The "want-to" in our own hearts to love God and to do what is right and pleasing to Him is what He is looking for, not our efforts to check boxes of self-righteousness.

Holy Spirit is always looking to bring out of us the best version of ourselves. Part of this process is unraveling the things we do (or possess) from our core identity. Our part is to invite the fire of His perfect love to burn away those hindrances—the dross—and bring forth the gold in who He has created us to be. God wants us, like Jesus' friend Martha, to identify ourselves by who we are, not by what we do. We are so much more than our professions, possessions, giftings, influence, social status, failures, or successes.

Our Triune Identity

Rene

As a young believer, I was taught in church that I could not trust my heart because the Bible says it is desperately wicked. This created an internal conflict because God had gotten hold of my desperately wicked heart outside of the church and promised to make something beautiful out of it. So what was I, wicked or beautiful?

The conflict was settled when Holy Spirit revealed that, apart from God, my heart *is* desperately wicked, but in Him it is oh, so beautiful. The stunning reality is that "dark, but lovely" are we to Him (Song of Songs 1:5). The voice that showed me my desperate need for a Savior was the same voice telling me I was made for greatness and that I could do all things through Christ who strengthens me (see Philippians 4:13). God saw something in me I could not fully see in myself. Once I started to see myself the way He sees me, through eyes of redemption and in the beauty of Christ's righteousness, I entered the discovery process of transformation, believing and receiving who He says I am, and no longer identifying with the past or with my old nature.

How we identify ourselves greatly determines who we become. When we receive Jesus Christ as Lord and Savior, we become "a new creation" (2 Corinthians 5:17), "the righteousness of God in Him" (2 Corinthians 5:21), "sealed with the Holy Spirit of promise" (Ephesians 1:13), and no longer identified with our sin. We become the saints of God, His holy people (see 1 Peter 2:9), having taken on a new nature (life), born again in His holiness and righteousness.

At the point of our conversion, we become painfully aware of our sin. The very weight of the consequences of our sin points us to our great need for our Lord and Savior, Jesus Christ. But once we trust in Him for salvation, we are no longer to carry the weight of our sin or identify with it, because Jesus took the penalty for it on the cross. We *were* sinners and *are* now saints, saved by grace through faith and transformed inwardly by the work of God's Spirit.

If we continue to identify ourselves with our old sin nature, we will be more prone to keep on sinning. But the apostle Paul wrote, "Count yourselves dead to sin but alive to God in Christ Jesus" (Romans 6:11 NIV). When we do, identifying ourselves with holiness and righteousness, we will be empowered to discern God's will and live a beautiful life, satisfying and perfect in His eyes (see Romans 12:1–2). This exchange from sinner to saint is vitally important in the transformation process as Holy Spirit reveals areas of sin that are hindering us, with which we must no longer identify.

God wants us to understand who we really are—that we have been adopted into His Kingdom family. From eternity past, this is our destiny. In Romans 8, Paul describes our position in the family of God:

All who are led by the Spirit of God are sons of God. For [the Spirit which] you have now received [is] not a spirit of slavery to put you once more in bondage to fear, but you have received the spirit of adoption [the Spirit producing sonship] in [the bliss of] which we cry, Abba (Father)! Father!

The Spirit Himself [thus] testifies together with our own spirit, [assuring us] that we are children of God. And if we are [His] children, then we are [His] heirs also; heirs of God and fellow heirs with Christ [sharing in His inheritance with Him]; only we must share in His sufferings if we are to share in His glory.

Romans 8:14–17 AMPC

The word *led* in verse 14 indicates a perpetual, moment-by-moment leading of Holy Spirit. The Passion Translation translates it this way: "The mature children of God are those who are moved by the impulses of the Holy Spirit." The phrase *impulses of the Holy Spirit* further indicates a greater sensitivity to His voice. It is about hearing His tender whispers and being obedient to His leading.

God is bringing sons and daughters back to His original intent. Just as Adam and Eve in the Garden of Eden were to take dominion and subdue the earth, so also is this our inheritance. Paul is saying that we will be revealed in our true identity with "the Spirit producing sonship" and adoption, who enables us to cry out, "Abba!" It is amazing!

The term *Abba* (or Daddy) invites us into a more tender relationship and intimate communion with Daddy God. The Father wants us to come to Him, knowing how approachable He is. When many might fear a backhand, He wants to show us Jesus' nail-pierced hands. He wants us to understand the depth of His love, the reality that He sent His only Son to reconcile us to Himself after the Fall. He longs for sons and daughters to understand that we can be restored to His original intent, that those who put their faith in His Son as

Savior will rule and reign with Him and be together with Him forever in His love.

God also wants us to understand that how we relate to each Person of the Godhead brings distinction and fullness to our supernatural identity:

- In relation to Father God, we are His beloved children, created in His image and likeness.
- In our union with Jesus Christ, we are identified as His Church, His Body, and His glorious Bride.
- And when we are filled with Holy Spirit, we are His habitation, empowered to live holy, set-apart lives, demonstrating the Kingdom of God with power.

Favored of the Father

You are the favored of the Father! God does not make mistakes, and He does not make junk; He makes masterpieces. Not a single person on earth is a mistake. Regardless of the circumstances around your birth, regardless of what you have been told, you were in the heart of God even before the foundations of the earth were laid.

Steven

My wonderful son, Justin, was born out of wedlock. In college my girlfriend became pregnant with our child. This was before I received Christ, but some of God's love was awakened in my heart through my son. The world would say he was illegitimate, a mistake. I tell you, that is not so. He is a blessing, amazing in every way! The mistake was mine and his mom's, but Justin was never a mistake. He is not illegitimate; he was in the heart of God even before the world was framed.

In the world's eyes, Jesus was considered illegitimate, conceived out of wedlock, but the truth is He was conceived in the heart of the Father to be the Savior of the world, born of a virgin who was overshadowed by Holy Spirit.

There is not a single illegitimate person on earth. You were created in God's image for greatness and destiny. We were all in the heart of God, and you were created in the love of God.

> He foreordained us (destined us, planned in love for us) to be adopted (revealed) as His own children through Jesus Christ, in accordance with the purpose of His will [because it pleased Him and was His kind intent].
>
> Ephesians 1:5 AMPC

You were created in love, for love, and you are the Father's pleasure. You are accepted; you are good enough. Why? Not because of your own effort or accomplishments, but because of the fire of perfect love. Through accepting that the blood of the Lamb of God was shed for you, you have been adopted as His child.

Think of yourself as a young child running to your father, crying out, "Daddy, Daddy, Daddy," and lifting up your arms to be picked up and held. You can come before your heavenly Father as freely as a child.

Keep doing this until you believe it. Keep saying, until you believe it, "Abba, Daddy, Father, I love You," and the Father's affections will be poured out on you. Every time you raise your hands to heaven and focus the gaze of your heart on the One who longs for you to draw close to Him, you have full access.

It is amazing that He has given us the privilege to be called children of God, "heirs of God and co-heirs with Christ" (Romans 8:17 NIV). Being a co-heir with Christ means that everything that belongs to the Father, He has given to His Son; if He has given it to the Son, then when we are born again, because of the shed blood and sacrifice of Jesus, we are in Christ and share with Him as co-heirs.

The Lord's desire at creation was for us to reign with Him side by side. Paul writes, "If we died with him, we will also live with him; if we endure, we will also reign with him" (2 Timothy 2:11–12 NIV). And God's people have been made "to be a kingdom and priests to serve our God, and they will reign on the earth" (Revelation 5:10 NIV).

God's plan of redemption was that we would do what Adam was instructed to do—take dominion, subdue the earth, and be fruitful and multiply. We are welcomed into the same reality. It is not something we are waiting for; forever starts today. Jesus said simply, "My Kingdom is at hand" (for example, see Matthew 4:17). It is right before you. It is ever present. It will always be there.

Look with wonder at the depth of the Father's marvelous love that he has lavished on us! He has called us and made us his very own beloved children. The reason the world doesn't recognize who we are is that they didn't recognize him. Beloved, we are God's children right now; however, it is not yet apparent what we will become. But we do know that when it is finally made visible, we will be just like him, for we will see him as he truly is. And all who focus their hope on him will always be purifying themselves, just as Jesus is pure.

1 John 3:1–3 TPT

Confidence in Intimacy

Remember the disciple John, who laid his head on Jesus' chest? He had such intimacy with Jesus, and such a deep revelation of His love, that he called himself "the disciple whom Jesus loved" (John 13:23 NIV). Imagine being with Jesus up close—so close and confident that you could lay your head on His chest, resting in His love and grace.

Imagine, as John leaned in and laid his head upon the chest of Jesus, that he would have been able to hear the rhythm of Jesus' heartbeat. He would probably have heard a soft echo of another heartbeat as well—the rhythm of the Father's heart. As John rested his head on Jesus' heart, Jesus was resting His own head upon the heart of the Father. The rhythm of their hearts would become one; and in this place of intimacy, John also would join the rhythm of the Father's heart and become one with them.

As we spend time leaning on the Lord, we become one with the Lord and His heartbeat and rhythm of love. This is your inheritance—to be one with Jesus, forged in the fire of perfect love. John said, "Consider the kind of extravagant love the Father has lavished on us" (1 John 3:1 VOICE). The word *lavish*, as we noted in the last chapter, means holding nothing back, but overflowing, extravagant, unconditional, enduring—and He has lavished His love on you.

We have had the privilege of seeing the power of God's lavish love transform our thirty wonderful Hope Home children in Ghana. Before they came to us, they had been orphaned, abandoned, severely neglected, or sold into slave labor and rescued with no home to return to. What unjust tragedies for these children! But God was bringing His justice through us.

At the opening of the Hope Home, we prayed for the spirit of adoption to be released over each one, and for the love of God to be unlocked within each heart. As they ran into our arms, we hugged and celebrated each child, declaring that each would know that he or she was not forgotten but accepted, adopted, and loved by Father God with an everlasting love. The Father had never stopped loving them, and He has a hope and a future for each one to walk confidently in.

When we taught the children what it means to be made brand-new in Jesus, and the importance of baptism, we asked by a show of hands who would like to be baptized. We were surprised and happy at the response of all thirty children. They all wanted to be baptized. So we made a trip to the Wli Waterfalls in the remote jungle of the Volta Region for baptisms. What a joyous day! As each one came up from the water, we declared over each of them an echo of what Father God proclaimed over His Son, Jesus, at His baptism: "This is my son/daughter, whom I love and with whom I am well pleased."

The transformation in their lives as they have been freed from the orphan mentality is amazing: from hoarding food to sharing freely with others; from months of physical fights every day to choosing to love and forgive one another; from telling lies and insults to speaking truth and kindness. As their hearts have been set free, they have begun to walk in dignity as the beloved children of God.

In the same way, the Father is waiting to embrace you and lavish on you His extravagant love. He is waiting for you to run into His arms and receive all that He has for you. He is so kind. He is always there for you. He will pick you up and restore you to wholeness. He will restore your identity and dignity so you can walk confidently today in the spirit of full acceptance.

The Affirmation of the Father

Before Jesus began His public ministry, He came to the Jordan River, where He asked His cousin John to baptize Him. As Jesus was coming up out of the water, suddenly the heavens opened, Holy Spirit descended on Him like a dove, and the Father's voice thundered, "This is my Son, whom I love; with him I am well pleased" (Matthew 3:17 NIV).

After that amazing proclamation of identity, Jesus was led to a place that would challenge those very words. He was led by Holy Spirit into the wilderness, where He was tempted for forty days. The wilderness is not always a bad place; in fact, it is often a place of encounter with God. But the enemy came when Jesus was hungry and tired, attacking the very declaration the Father had just made over Him: "*If* You are the Son of God. . . ." Rather than be swayed by the challenge of the enemy, however, Jesus let the words of His Father reverberate through His innermost being, quoting the words of Scripture back to the devil and remaining steadfast in His identity as the Son of God.

Imagine, if the enemy tried to get Jesus to question His identity, how much more does he try to release noisy lies over those created in God's image? The truth is, we are beloved children of the Most High God, and we are immersed in His lavish love.

Later in Jesus' ministry, He worked to uproot the mentality of slavery, and even the wrong sense of servanthood. Paul, Timothy, James, Peter, and Jude all called themselves bondservants of Christ, meaning that they chose to serve Him with a bond rooted so strongly in His love that it could be broken only by their death. No longer were they bound to a slavery mindset, but to the freedom of servanthood. God wants to bring us into the truth of our identity that we are no longer slaves held bound by sin or religious duty, but He is calling us to the higher place to be with Him in love.

Receive these words of Jesus:

"Slaves have no permanent standing in a family, like a son does, for a son is a part of the family forever. So if the Son sets you free from sin, then become a true son and be unquestionably free!"

John 8:35–36 TPT

"I have never called you 'servants,' because a master doesn't confide in his servants, and servants don't always understand what the master is doing. But I call you my most intimate and cherished friends, for I reveal to you everything that I've heard from my Father."

John 15:15 TPT

Jesus is saying to you today, "I don't call you a servant or a slave, so don't live like one. But I have called you an intimate friend, for I reveal to you everything that I've heard from My Father."

And the Father is declaring over you today: "You are My son, My daughter, whom I love, and with whom I am well pleased." He is not ashamed of you, but proud of you. The more you believe this, the more you will be free to be you!

Your Identity in Christ

You were born for such a time as this. God calls you His own and invites you to be one of those who will usher in the greatest move of Holy Spirit the earth has ever known. God's army is on the rise, and you must know who you are.

But the battle around identity is fierce. Many things—in the world, in our pasts, and in ourselves—try to define us. The enemy knows that once the Body of Christ gets hold of who we really are, *game over*!

When we walk in our identity as children of God and saints in His Kingdom, knowing we are loved by our heavenly Father, four primary characteristics begin to show themselves in our lives: boldness, rest, inheritance, and Kingdom authority. Let's look briefly at each.

Boldness

Rene

Some people are bold by personality, like Steven. He releases great faith through that boldness. I am gentle and contemplative by nature. But years back, I desired to be bold in releasing faith. So I prayed and asked God to help me to be bolder.

Around that time, our daughter was a confident three-year-old, which presented challenges. Although Elizabeth was petite, she was large and in charge. I admired her boldness but knew we needed God's help in redirecting her strong will.

One night at church, while a guest speaker was sharing, Elizabeth decided to make her presence known. She darted up front and began walking back and forth, head held high, with a stride that said, "I own this place." As I tried to get her attention and began to reach for her, the guest speaker stopped mid-sentence from behind the pulpit and said, "Do you know why your daughter is so bold?"

Shocked at the attention and slightly embarrassed, I froze in place.

He answered his own question quickly: "Because she knows she is loved."

His answer surprised me with the weight it carried. And as I pondered his words in my heart, God's Spirit continued to bring revelation.

Elizabeth's strong will *did* need to be redirected. But as for me, I did not need to pray for more boldness, or try to be bolder, but simply *become* bolder by posturing my heart to receive more of My heavenly Father's love. Receiving and becoming took the striving out of trying to change myself; it brought the ease of simply receiving and relying on more of God's perfect love.

Rest

Resting in our identity means we are no longer striving or trying to do things for God, but resting in His unconditional love and doing things *with* Him. Heavy burdens are lifted as we carry things with Him (since His yoke is easy and His burden is light, according to Matthew 11:30). When you know you are loved by God and can sense His approval, you can come into rest instead of needing approval or feeling that you are being driven by a religious taskmaster. From a confident and restful state of *being*, we get to *do* amazing things with God, as the beauty of His perfect love is expressed through our lives.

Inheritance

Rene

We see throughout the Word of God, going back to Jacob and Esau and earlier, that receiving an inheritance is important to Father God. It is something we should value and expect and rejoice in as His children. But it was a foreign concept to me in my upbringing, and it has been greatly lost in Western culture—although Steven and I have seen it still being lived out beautifully in the fabric of other cultures.

When we began our ministry as missionaries, God showed Himself faithful in providing for us in unusual and undeniable ways. My expectation and faith, however, were for "just enough," and that is what we received. As beautiful as it was to see God provide outside of our own talents and gifts, He revealed to me that I was operating from an orphan spirit in the area of provision. Then He led me to understand and receive His provision through the lens of sonship and daughtership, receiving our inheritance from Him and trusting in His more-than-enough abundance.

We did nothing differently in serving through ministry, but simply postured our hearts differently; by doing so, we have seen an amazing increase in the inward reality of receiving the glorious riches of Christ Jesus, and in natural resources as well.

Kingdom Authority

Our heavenly Father longs for us to receive all He has provided through the extravagant gift of His Son, Jesus, who gave it all so we could receive the fullness of what His death and resurrection purchased: salvation of our souls and the ability to become living expressions of Christ on the earth, demonstrating the greater reality of the Kingdom of God.

Jesus said, "All authority has been given to Me in heaven and on earth" (Matthew 28:18). In the name of Jesus, we have authority "to heal sicknesses and to cast out demons" (Mark 3:15) and "over all the power of the enemy" (Luke 10:19). But we must be faith-filled and courageous enough to believe and walk in our authority by cultivating a lifestyle of supernatural power. From our identity as children of God, it is important for us to demonstrate the power of His Kingdom and to take dominion. Exercising our authority in obedience to the Great Commission—"Go, therefore . . ." (Matthew 28:19)—is true humility, expressed not in shrinking from our confident stance as sons and daughters of God, but in laying down our lives in surrender to His perfect will and rising up in resurrection power.

As perfect love casts out fear from our lives, we become fearless. It is actually Satan who is fearful of what happens when a generation lives out this reality on earth. When we know who we are and whose we are, and that heaven backs us up, we can be fearless and bold witnesses.

Journey into Perfect Love

Review the following list to help determine if you are identifying with your old nature as a sinner or if you have come into agreement with your new nature as a saint. Are you:

- Feeling dirty (sinful) instead of clean (washed)?
- Feeling guilty (condemned) instead of innocent (pure)?
- More sin-conscious than holy-conscious?
- Feeling unworthy or "less than" rather than as God's chosen treasure?
- More aware of failures than successes?
- Trying harder (striving) rather than relying more (thriving)?
- Fearful of never being good enough rather than believing you are fully accepted?
- Hard on yourself instead of empowered by grace?
- Hating yourself because you see sin as a part of you rather than hating it as something that is no longer part of your new nature? (We need to hate sin but love ourselves.)

We all have struggles, but it is important that we do not find identity in them.

Here are some examples, followed by declarations of truth that we encourage you to say out loud:

- You may make mistakes, but you are not a mistake. "I am God's unique masterpiece!"
- You may struggle with addiction, but you are not defined by it. "I am made to crave the presence of God and to be continually filled!"
- You may be in a dark place, struggling with fear or depression, but these characteristics do not define you. They are not *your* demons, *your* fear, *your* disease. They have trespassed and squatted in your life, and it is time to serve the eviction notice. "I am a child of the light, made to radiate God's glory!"
- You may struggle with a demonic stronghold, but you are not demonic. "I am a freedom fighter made to be free and set the captives free!"

Father God, I thank You for the fire of Your perfect love at work unraveling lies and misconceptions from my identity. Burn up all that hinders Your perfect love from being expressed in its fullness in my life, and reveal the truth of who I am, according to the finished work of the cross and my original design.

For Supernatural Identity spoken over you, accompanied by the prophetic music, see our complete IMMERSE soaking series available on our website www.globalpresence.com/PerfectLove.

SIX

Radiating the Inner Fire

All nations will come to your light; mighty kings will come to see your radiance.

Isaiah 60:3 NLT

Steven

A few years ago a friend of mine returned from Wales in the United Kingdom and brought back two gifts for me from his travels. One was a book on the Welsh revival, the awakening and outpouring of Holy Spirit in the early twentieth century; the other was a piece of coal that would have been in the ground at the very time of that revival.

In 1904, just prior to the Azusa Street revival in Los Angeles, a young man named Evan Roberts, about twenty-six years old, became the catalyst for the Welsh revival. Evan was a son of a coal miner. His parents were sincere believers and taught their children the importance of a relationship with Jesus and a passion for His Word. While Evan was still young, his father suffered an injury from a mining accident, so Evan was taken out of school to help in the mines. As a result, the family traditions of mining and the love of Scripture memorization were passed down to Evan. It was said he was never seen without his Bible. The Man of fire, Jesus, got hold of the young coal miner and set him on fire.

Revival came. Not only did his world change, but the whole world would never be the same.

Because of the awakening in Wales, I have a proclivity for that piece of coal. To me, it represents fuel for the fire of revival and my longing for God to do it again in our day. God is looking for fuel for the fire—not only those who will burn, but those who will embrace the intense pressure in the midst of the flame.

Coal is composed of carbon, and it burns nicely as fuel; but place carbon under intense heat and pressure, and something far more valuable than coal is produced: diamonds. The chemical makeup of coal and diamonds is identical. But the difference between a chunk of coal and a diamond is in the arrangement of the molecules, which is why coal and diamonds differ in formation, hardness, and appearance. Coal has disorganized layers of molecules and many impurities, whereas a diamond, due to intense heat and pressure, has an organized molecular structure.

Our lives, before we know Jesus, are like that piece of coal—dark, full of impurities, and unable to refract light. But in Christ, we are pure and righteous in our spiritual structure or DNA.

Making Diamonds Out of Us

When jewelers look at a cut diamond through a magnifying "loupe," they see a unique sparkle and inner radiance, which is called the inner fire. That is exactly what God desires to produce in us. The colored beauty and inner fire are what make diamonds rare, precious, mysterious, and desirable.

Diamonds are tokens of love that have represented romantic passion throughout history. They have unique characteristics that set them apart from other gemstones and give them value beyond price. Distinct in personality and character, no two diamonds are ever the same.

We, too, are unique, precious, and desirable, made to shine with the light of Jesus. We are beautiful tokens of the love that ignited the passion of Jesus to lay down His life to restore us to the Father, now and for eternity.

And when we receive the baptism with Holy Spirit, we reveal an inner fire, just like a diamond. We are made to be the radiance of Christ for the world to see. He lives in us as believers through His Spirit, but we must undergo a process much like the process that forms diamonds, so we begin to reflect the radiance and splendor and glory of Jesus, the King of the universe.

Natural diamonds are formed over a significant amount of time, deep within the earth's mantle, under conditions of intense heat and pressure that cause carbon atoms to crystallize.

Just as a diamond takes time to form, so is it with our lives. There is a grace-filled process in which Holy Spirit transforms us from the inside out. God knows that this process will take time. He is patient with us. He enjoys the process, and never loses sight of the diamond being formed. Neither should we! The work of God's Spirit happens in deep places within us, and we must go low in yielding to the process.

It takes our entering the fire of His love and allowing Him to burn off whatever diminishes our radiance—things like distractions, shame, addiction, depression, and unworthiness. Allowing Him to press us from all angles begins to create a molecular change so that we become more and more like Him.

We must remember, then, that when the heat and pressure are turned up in our lives, they will produce something pure and beautiful. The Lord purifies our hearts by tests and trials, and He uses them to make us strong and durable. "You know that when your faith is tested it stirs up in you the power of endurance" (James 1:3 TPT). And Paul wrote:

> Even in times of trouble we have a joyful confidence, knowing that our pressures will develop in us patient endurance. And patient endurance will refine our character, and proven character leads us back to hope.
>
> Romans 5:3–4 TPT

Tests and trials are rarely enjoyable, but how we view and respond in these uncomfortable situations make them great opportunities for growth. When under pressure, we may be tempted to run or take the easy way out. But we must embrace the pressure, or we will miss the growth it brings. God never gives up on us, so we should not give up on ourselves. The only way we lose is if we quit. Remember, we are diamonds in the rough; it might get rough, but we are still diamonds!

The cut of a diamond is one of the most important quality factors because it determines the brilliance of the stone—how it refracts light. A jeweler cutting facets on a diamond is like when God begins to cut away things in us that hinder the refraction of His radiance and beauty. With great delight, He never loses sight of the radiance He is bringing forth in us, and neither should we.

Remember, all diamonds are unique, not perfect. Since they are formed underground through enormous pressure and heat, natural blemishes and inclusions (small imperfections) are inevitable. In most cases, they do not affect a diamond's beauty since most cannot be seen with the naked eye. It is the same with our weaknesses and flaws—they do not lessen our value or hinder God's perfect love from shining through us. But the enemy will try to exploit our weaknesses if we are not careful to protect and value what God is doing in our lives.

Diamonds form as carbon atoms under high temperature and pressure, and bond together. In the same way, when we as members of the Body of Christ enter the fire together, we bond with one another. God's desire for His Church is to be in the fire together. Otherwise we would become like a single molecule burning on our own and would eventually burn out. But when we are in the fire with other believers, the closeness, along with the pressure, makes less room for sin to darken our beauty, and for more light to get refracted.

The densely linked molecular structure of a diamond makes it one of the hardest naturally occurring substances on earth. When God brings the Church together in the fire, we find a resilience and strength that makes it difficult for the enemy to break through.

The diamonds that lie deep within the earth come up through volcanic eruptions. What God forms in the deep places, He brings forth in resurrection power. Just as Jesus was "in the heart of the earth" (Matthew 12:40) after He was crucified, He was raised with power—and the same is true with us.

What a beautiful opportunity we are given as we yield to the transformation process! We are the workmanship of God's hands. He is the gem cutter who, with great precision and care, forms and fashions us to shine brightly in a dark world.

You are God's chosen treasure—priests who are kings, a spiritual "nation" set apart as God's devoted ones. He called you out of darkness to experience his marvelous light, and now he claims you as his very own. He did this so that you would broadcast his glorious wonders throughout the world.

1 Peter 2:9 TPT

The Brilliance of the Inner Fire

To showcase the beauty and radiance of a diamond, a jeweler will place it against a backdrop of black velvet. That is what God does with us. He sets us against the backdrop of darkness, where we radiate and refract all the dimensions of our good, good Father. Like the brilliance of diamonds showcased on black velvet, like shining stars in the canopy of the night sky, we are the radiance of Christ against the backdrop of a darkened world.

Our part is to stay in the light of His countenance. When we turn our gaze away from God, striving to change ourselves, we reflect manmade religion, artificial, lacking in both brilliance and resilience. But as we keep our gaze toward heaven, the light of God's face shines on us, displaying our inner fire and the brilliance of Christ.

Only as we embrace God's grace in the transformation process will the genuine work of Christ be seen in our lives. It is not the synthetic work of human beings, but the authentic work of God. We have been created by the master jeweler, unique and uniquely His, created in His image.

The rich young ruler recognized the inner fire in Jesus and saw the nature of Father God. Jesus was the exact replication of His Father. This is why the young man called Him good. Look at their exchange:

> As He was going out on the road, one came running, knelt before Him, and asked Him, "Good Teacher, what shall I do that I may inherit eternal life?" So Jesus said to him, "Why do you call Me good? No one is good but One, that is, God."
>
> Mark 10:17–18

That is the reason Jesus came to planet earth—to represent His good Father and to show the world how good God is. The rich young ruler saw something in Jesus that was different from others, a pure goodness, yet he limited the revelation of Jesus as Messiah by referring to Jesus as *Teacher*.

Jesus provoked him to think differently by asking him, "Why do you call Me good?" He asked the question not to minimize His Father's goodness in Himself, but to indicate that His very goodness revealed that He is God. He was affirming His own deity. "I am" is what Jesus was saying.

The Good News is that

> God anointed Jesus of Nazareth with the Holy Spirit and with power, who went about doing good and healing all who were oppressed by the devil, for God was with Him.
>
> Acts 10:38

Jesus is good and did good because He is God.

Moses was another who possessed the inner fire of God, because he chose to draw near to God. As we look at his life with the Israelites, meandering in the wilderness for forty years, we hear the Israelites complaining the entire time, even though they were led by a cloud by day and a fire by night. During this time, we see Moses reflecting God's glory so strongly that it radiated visibly from his face.

The Israelites had the same choice as Moses in drawing near to God, but they refused, insisting that Moses go on their behalf. As a result, the Israelites merely observed the outer pillar of fire rather than possess the inner flame.

> Even the ministry that was characterized by chiseled letters on stone tablets came with a dazzling measure of glory, though it produced death. The Israelites couldn't bear to gaze on the glowing face of Moses because of the radiant splendor shining from his countenance—a glory destined to fade away. Yet how much more radiant is this new and glorious ministry of the Spirit that shines from us!
>
> 2 Corinthians 3:7–8 TPT

Let's not be like the Israelites, observing only the outer fire. Let's be mindful to keep first love burning and the fire on the altar of our hearts ablaze. As we choose to tend to the inner flame, both individually and collectively, God will bring about a manifestation similar to what Moses experienced in the Tent of Meeting, where fire, smoke, glory, and the weightiness of His grace and love will come forth and be made manifest to His people. It is our turn to embrace the inner flame.

We, Steven and Rene, have seen the manifestation of God's glory clouds a couple of times in our ministry.

Steven

One time in particular, we were in the last few hours of a twenty-seven-hour worship time. The atmosphere was supercharged with the weighty presence of the Lord, with revelation and the release of the new song and prophetic glory. At one point, when we were praying the Word back to the Lord and worshiping in the Spirit, I felt His overwhelming pleasure. A weight came over me as I had my eyes closed. In my mind's eye, I was looking into the fiery eyes of Jesus.

As I opened my eyes, everything seemed cloudy. At first, I thought my eyes needed to adjust, but as I looked, I began to see a cloud form above my head and begin to swirl and grow. Wondering if I was the only one seeing it, I looked over at our worship team. They were also seeing the cloud billow and grow. My eyes teared up as I felt the weighty love of God fill the room. The cloud swirled for about two hours.

At one point, our sound man left the soundboard and came running up, sliding face first under the cloud, weeping under the swirling, weighty love. At another point a young woman came into the room to soak in His presence. As she walked through the door at the back of the room, she said, "It was as if I hit a barrier—a thickening of the atmosphere that I had to press through." As she did, she saw the glory cloud and came running to worship under His weighty love.

All of us were overcome by His weighty goodness, mercy, and love. We were not worshiping the cloud, but the One who made the cloud—the same God who created the cloud in the wilderness for Israel in their journey to the Promised Land.

Don't try to figure it out—just get into the cloud because His presence is powerful. God is looking for those who will tend to His presence and that fiery flame of love, through which we can demonstrate His goodness and victory, and go forth with boldness.

The Higher Perspective

The apostle Paul understood bold faith, and much of it came from having the right perspective in the midst of intense pressure.

Paul was lashed, beaten with rods, stoned, thrown into prison, shipwrecked, and left for dead. But he called these trials "light momentary affliction" (2 Corinthians 4:17 ESV). He also said, "I consider that the sufferings of this present time are not worthy to be compared with the glory which shall be revealed in us" (Romans 8:18).

The inner fire inside Paul enabled him, in the midst of trials, to see and reflect God's goodness, because his vision was a heavenly vision. He was in the world (momentary affliction) but not of the world (seated in heavenly places). The Kingdom reality is greater than the earthly reality.

Someone else with a higher perspective was the prophet Elisha. When enemies were all around him, and his servant was distressed at what he saw in the natural realm, Elisha had eyes to see beyond the veil for the higher perspective. He saw "the hills full of horses and chariots of fire all around Elisha" (2 Kings 6:17 NIV). Warring angels of holy passion who had been in God's presence were there, dispatched by heaven, because Elisha did not keep silent. He was a praying, seeing, and decreeing prophet.

Elisha's vision and Paul's higher perspective are also available to us. Too often we get stuck under the weight of the issues and troubles going on in our lives, even from past seasons. We can get so focused on the bad things that we miss the good things God is doing—and that He is for us. When we pray, circumstances shift and a higher reality is made manifest.

God wants to take us to the higher place, where we are seated with Him and in Him. He wants to bring us into a fresh encounter with His goodness so we can experience Him and what He is doing beyond the veil. That is what will sustain us. And this vision is not just a one-time thing; it becomes a lifestyle, regardless of situations and circumstances going on around us and in the world.

God is inviting you to ascend the stairway of glory, revelation, and freedom to the higher place. But you must go before Him with boldness. You have an amazing opportunity to "come boldly to the throne of grace" (Hebrews 4:16) and enter His presence with thanksgiving and praise. This unlocks realms so you can run in and celebrate the victory Jesus has given you.

Keeping the Inner Fire Burning

God's goodness gets us through the trials and into victory. Testimonies are powerful. They are remembrance stones, like diamonds, releasing the radiance of the good things God has done, so when times of trouble come, we can look back and say, "Look what God did for me here. He's going to do it again."

Steven

When Rene and I were stuck in the mire of sin and selfishness, when our hearts were far from Him, God apprehended us with His love and mercy. That is God's goodness.

In Africa, we prayed for a baby boy who was raised from the dead in the very place where human sacrifice was done. That is God's goodness. We have seen blind eyes opened and deaf ears unstopped in response to our prayers. That is God's goodness. We have seen thousands saved, healed, and delivered. That is God's goodness. My mom passed on from cancer, and God comforted my heart and strengthened my faith to continue to believe. That is God's goodness. My dad was later healed of cancer. That is God's goodness.

God is breaking in to ignite the inner fire, and as He breaks in, He wants to break out.

Rene

We want to cooperate with the work of God's fire and not hinder it. One way we hinder it is by harboring offense. As the inner fire is at work, shifting and changing us from the inside out, we must be aware of when our hearts are becoming offended with God. He often does things in a way and with timing that we do not expect or understand, which can lead to frustration—and, when left unchecked, offense.

God's Spirit usually shows up in the "midnight hour" with revelation light that pierces the darkness and brings breakthrough. Jesus, our Savior, came into the world and left this world in a much different way than those watching for Him and journeying with Him expected. Those who yielded their expectations were transformed; those who did not betrayed Him.

I pray that we learn to yield our expectations and trust God in the midst of uncertainty. The following story was one such time for me.

When God called Steven and me into full-time vocational ministry, it meant letting go of the modeling agency I owned. The music ministry we were leading was exploding, as we said earlier, and many people were getting saved, healed, and delivered. It was getting to the point that we could not manage both career and ministry. So when God made it clear that it was time to let the agency go, promising that I would become an ambassador of His beauty, I thought we were ready to let go of everything to follow His call and that we would be incredibly blessed. After all, we were giving it up for Jesus. Right?

We *were* blessed—but in a much different way than I expected. God blessed us with a time in the wilderness. That did not feel like a blessing! I did not understand that God is more interested in the inward shift than in my outward obedience.

Everything began to be stripped from our lives—where we had found our identity; where we put our security; the circle of people we ran with; the familiarity of our lifestyle in the modeling industry. Our income went down to a quarter of what it had been. People who knew us were questioning our decision because, even from the outside, things were not looking so good.

I began to question everything. If this was God's plan, then why was everything so hard and seemed the opposite of His blessing? I was also concerned for our son, Justin, who was ten years old. His lifestyle was changing with ours. We no longer had discretionary money to spend on him, and we were no longer hanging out with professional athletes, celebrities, and models from the agency. All our savings, including Justin's college fund, were gone. How could I explain it to him when I did not understand myself what God was doing after we had given it all up for Him? I thought we were ruining Justin's life.

As the pressure mounted—even our vehicles were breaking down—I was offended at God. We were following Him wholeheartedly and everything was getting worse, not better. I cried, "God, this is ridiculous! I can do something about this. I can easily go out and get a job."

The Spirit of God answered tenderly yet sternly, *Yes, you can do something about this, just as Jesus could have done something about it when He was on the cross. He could have called on the angels to save Him, but for the greater purpose, He endured. I am asking you to endure for the greater purpose I am working out in and through you. It is not about what you do for Christ but about what He did for you. Your life and obedience must be in response to what has already been done on your behalf.*

When I poured out my heart to God my concerns about our son, He made my heart a promise: *Justin doesn't understand right now, but he will someday, and it will be part of a great strength I will build in him. He will see my favor and provision in his life.*

When the Spirit of God takes us to a deeper revelation of the cross, that puts an end to all pity parties. I wept in the beauty of repentance, asking God to help me to embrace what He wanted to do in my heart. That is the moment I started to embrace the crucified life, and I began to learn what it is to release our children to God in following His will.

As I discovered our true riches in Christ, our earthly riches began to be restored, and we experienced God's provision in miraculous ways. God's promise that our son would see His favor and provision came to pass as Justin received both academic and football scholarships, which covered his college tuition in biomedical engineering. He is now a man after God's heart, with a beautiful wife and children who all love the Lord, and tremendous favor in his career.

The key was an inward yielding of our hearts and minds to God's will and learning to trust His leadership in our lives, no matter what the outward circumstances looked like.

I have learned that as God walks with us through the valley of the shadow of death—whatever kind of death we are experiencing—if we do not fear the opinions of others, but rely on the comfort of His good leadership and the strength of His discipline, we will eventually come into the wide open spaces of the abundant life in Him.

If God is going to pour out His Spirit, the anointing will come through intense heat and pressure. This, as we have seen, is how diamonds are made. Many of us have lived in a comfortable bubble, but Holy Spirit is the Comforter, not a peaceful environment. (Remember that friends in many other countries are being persecuted for their faith in Jesus. We will talk about this in chapter 9.)

God wants to be our all in all. I have done a word study on *all* in Greek, Aramaic, and Hebrew, and *all* means "all." I am joking, but it is true: God wants all of us. When we give Him all of us, He gives us all of Him.

And it is not a fantasy that, when you have put your faith in Jesus, you can experience the endless love of God cascading into your heart through Holy Spirit. You were made to live in His presence and to burn with an inner fire. He is making you one of the bright and shining ones, and He will put you against the tapestry of darkness so you can radiate and beam forward the goodness of our Father. Then the multicolored dimensions of His favor and grace will be released to a lost, dark, and dying world that has been created for His presence.

Journey into Perfect Love

Reflect on the following questions:

- What are some things in your life that God might want to remove so He can begin to shape, create, and polish you to display His radiance and beauty?
- Can you still approach God confidently—despite the pressures, hard circumstances, and unknowns in your life—as a loving and good Father? If not, what areas in

your life need His healing touch to bring the revelation of Him as a good Father?

- God is looking for those who will tend to His presence and cultivate the inner fire. Will you be one who boldly approaches the throne of grace, going up to the higher places to be one of His bright and shining ones?

Join us in declaring this poem out loud:

> Like the shining stars in the canopy of the night sky,
> like the brilliance of diamonds showcased on black velvet,
> I am the radiance of Christ against the backdrop of a
>   darkened world.
> The inner fire inside consumes me with a love so perfect,
> so pure, I am undone by its majestic power.
> I am being transformed as I yield to the brilliance
> of this most vehement flame.
>
> Poem by Rene Springer

SEVEN

A Presence-Centered Life

One thing I have desired of the Lord, that will I seek: that I
may dwell in the house of the Lord all the days of my life, to
behold the beauty of the Lord, and to inquire in His temple.

Psalm 27:4

Steven

Through the birth of our daughter, Elizabeth, the Lord showed
Rene and me a profound prophetic picture of what would mark
a generation.

Elizabeth arrived four weeks early. And instead of being born
with her chin down and the top of her head coming through the
birth canal, she was born with her chin up, face first. Coming
through face first provided no give, causing excruciating pain
for both Rene and our baby.

After I cut the cord, Rene was holding her, but Elizabeth's
face was extremely bruised and swollen, and one side of her

face was drooping. Another doctor was called in to assess the trauma. Both doctors expressed concern that her face would remain partially paralyzed.

We would not accept that report.

I asked to hold our little girl, and held her close to me, face to face, declaring the greater reality of the power of God to bring healing and restoration. As I prayed, a smile spread across her face, and all the drooping miraculously disappeared.

The doctors expressed amazement at the shift (and the smile on her face), continued with their initial examination, then took her to the neonatal intensive care unit (NICU) because she was four weeks premature and because of her birth trauma. She would remain in the NICU for several days. We did not know this would be the last time we would be able to hold our daughter for days.

I went back and forth between being with my wife and my daughter, reaching into the isolette to touch our precious girl, whom I longed to hold.

On that first night, as the hospital staff told me it was time to go, I knew there was no way I was going to leave my little girl. I was staying.

Then Father God said to me, *Don't worry. I've got her.*

He opened my eyes to see a massive angel standing at her head, watching over her with tender attention. I looked and saw at every isolette in the NICU an angel standing and keeping watch over each and every precious child. With this assurance and peace, I was able to trust the Father to take care of her.

Elizabeth and Rene recovered fully, and our daughter is now an amazing light in this generation.

The Lord showed us, through Elizabeth's birth, many parallels to what those in her generation have faced, and what the redemptive purposes and plans of the Lord are for them.

Beholding God's Beauty

The enemy wants take out the young people of this generation with trauma, causing paralysis and keeping them from their destiny. But the greater reality is that this is a face-first generation, one who will be found gazing continually into the loving eyes of the Father. Their faces will be heaven-bound, and no trauma will keep them from the amazing calling and destiny the Lord has for them. It is His voice that will cause all things to come into alignment.

Let it be our prayer and resounding cry that this generation be found gazing on the face of the Father, encountering the beauty and majesty of His presence, just as David did in his days on earth. He beheld the beauty of God in the face of trials and the noise of the accuser.

Here is his Psalm 27 in *The Message* translation:

Light, space, zest—that's GOD! So, with him on my side I'm fearless, afraid of no one and nothing. When vandal hordes ride down ready to eat me alive, those bullies and toughs fall flat on their faces. When besieged, I'm calm as a baby. When all hell breaks loose, I'm collected and cool.

I'm asking GOD for one thing, only one thing: to live with him in his house my whole life long. I'll contemplate his beauty; I'll study at his feet. That's the only quiet, secure place in a noisy world, the perfect getaway, far from the buzz of traffic.

God holds me head and shoulders above all who try to pull me down. I'm headed for his place to offer anthems that will raise the roof! Already I'm singing God-songs; I'm making music to GOD.

Listen, GOD, I'm calling at the top of my lungs: "Be good to me! Answer me!" When my heart whispered, "Seek God," my whole being replied, "I'm seeking him!" Don't hide from me now!

You've always been right there for me; don't turn your back on me now. Don't throw me out, don't abandon me; you've always kept the door open. My father and mother walked out and left me, but GOD took me in.

Point me down your highway, GOD: direct me along a well-lighted street; show my enemies whose side you're on. Don't throw me to the dogs, those liars who are out to get me, filling the air with their threats.

I'm sure now I'll see God's goodness in the exuberant earth. Stay with GOD! Take heart. Don't quit. I'll say it again: Stay with GOD.

Most likely David wrote Psalm 27 when he was somewhere between seventeen and twenty years old. We know his approximate age because he was running from the enemies who wanted to devour him. David was a worshiper who had caught the attention of heaven because of his simplicity and burning heart after God. The prophet Samuel anointed him king when David was around fifteen, and God's Spirit came heavily upon him. But for about fifteen years, King Saul pursued David, trying to kill him.

Regardless of what was going on around this young man—a lion and a bear attacking his father's sheep; a blasphemous giant challenging the army of Israel; the king chasing him down to kill him—David held fast in knowing and proclaiming God's love.

God wants us to worship simply, like children unhindered by religion, understanding that we are adored, the true objects of the affection of His heart. David grabbed hold of these truths early on. He was fearless and confident; he knew who he was and was not afraid of anyone. Listen to Psalm 27:1: "The LORD is my light and my salvation; whom shall I fear? The LORD is the strength of my life; of whom shall I be afraid?"

David understood that God was his all in all. How did he know? By spending time with the Lord, experiencing God's presence from the time he was a shepherd boy in the fields. With a simple harp and an audience of One, David created an atmosphere in which God could speak to him, reveal His love, and convince him that, with God at his side, he was invincible.

God wants to infuse that reality into your innermost being, too. With Him at your side, *you* are invincible. Romans 8:31 says, "If God is for us, who can be against us?" You are invincible because the power of Jesus Christ is in you, and He is the hope of glory. If you have said yes to Him and confessed Him as Savior and Lord, you are hedged in behind and before. He is with you all the time.

During the years that David was being pursued by the murderous King Saul, his heart's desire was to "dwell in the house of the LORD all the days of my life, to gaze on the beauty of the LORD and to seek him in his temple" (Psalm 27:4 NIV). David wanted to live in God's house all the days of his life, to contemplate God's beauty, and to study at His feet. This pursuit of intimacy is available to us all.

David saw something else, too, something a thousand years in the future—the reality of King Jesus, the uncreated One, stepping out of the realm of heaven and coming down to weak and broken people, to pull them out of the muck and mire and entanglements of sin. David thanked God repeatedly for His salvation, and was fixated on remaining in God's presence forever, being His friend, being His son, and beholding the One with eyes of fire. Regardless of the schemes of the enemy, David was not going to lose track, lose hope, or lose focus.

The Weapon of Praise

There is a real enemy after you as well. Your trials and tribulations may not be the same as David's. You probably do not have people trying to eat your flesh. But there is a real war going on in the heavenly realm. You have probably experienced demonic attacks and the assault of the enemy coming at you from the left and from the right. He hates you and everything about you because you look like your Father in heaven.

It is interesting that not until you are born again and touched by God's love does the reality of spiritual warfare come against you, because now you know too much.

The enemy wants to keep your focus away from Almighty God and on your mistakes and weaknesses—the way you sometimes trip and fall and blow it. On the other hand, God sees you in the fullness of how He created you and in your destiny. The truth is that in your weakness you are made strong (see 2 Corinthians 12:9–10).

We have a wrong assessment of who we are, who God is, and who the enemy is. We give him too much credit. But when we consider that "the Son of God came to destroy the works of the devil" (1 John 3:8 NLT), we will readjust our focus, and see and worship the uncreated One who is unshakable.

That is why worship and praise are our greatest weapons of warfare. David said in Psalm 22:3 that God is "enthroned in the praises of Israel." When we lift up the name of Jesus together, God comes into our midst in a fresh way. And as we continue to press in, we will experience a weightiness and change in the atmosphere—more of His presence.

David wanted to build a house for the Lord (although it would be his son Solomon who would build the Temple years later). But God created you and me to *be* the house. There is an awakening in our generation, and we will create "thin places" for His presence. But the reality is, *you* are the place for His presence. You are the house God is looking for. You are His resting place. So rest in Him!

When we see God as He is, an all-consuming fire, He will consume the impurities in us and all those things that come against us. He is looking for a generation with a burning heart like His, which has tasted and seen the goodness of His love and is taking that reality to the world.

Regardless of what you are going through, understand that God is for you. He wants to take you to the deeper places to understand His kindness and His loving heart.

Encountering Waves

Steven

I was in a meeting once in which the speaker shared about the love and fear of the Lord. As the message continued, a movement suddenly started in the back of the room. I began to hear voices crying, "O God! O God!" It was like a wave that came from the back of the room all the way to the front. A gateway had opened for God.

Before I could say a word, I was on the floor weeping. A weighty fear of the Lord had entered the room. I was pressed to the floor. Those around me were also weeping. We understood the weightiness of God—His vastness, His greatness, His goodness, His love that cannot be contained. His presence was so heavy, it was as if the breath was being pushed out of my lungs. There was so much light emanating from the Lord's presence that I saw the dark places in my heart. I had not even known those dark places were in there. Now I could see the evil intent of my heart, apart from His loving presence.

No sooner did the wave of the fear of the Lord dissipate than another wave came from the front of the room. It was as if this wave hit the front wall and splashed back. Have you ever been to the ocean where there are huge sea walls? The waves come crashing in and then rebound off the sea wall. That is exactly what this experience felt like. But this time, as the wave crashed back, it was a wave of the Father's weighty, fiery love.

I was so overwhelmed by the kindness of the Father that His perfect, unfailing love brought restoration and hope. Boldness and confidence arose within me that I was loved, fully accepted in Him, and that I could do all things through Christ. I understood that He really liked me, that His affections were toward me and for me. I was overwhelmed by the spirit of adoption and the power of His unfailing love. My response was to lift my hands in worship as tears of joy streamed down my face.

A few minutes later, another wave came from the back of the room, a wave of the fear of the Lord. Once again I was on my face, crushed to the floor, weeping, with a penitent heart filled with sorrow, seeing in my soul my own wickedness apart from God's presence. Moments later, a wave of the Father's love came crashing back, affirming His love and my royal position as a dearly loved son.

This went on for about forty-five minutes. The entire room was overwhelmed with wave after wave of the power and presence of the Lord. It was like a chiropractic adjustment as my life came into alignment with the fear of the Lord and His unfailing, fiery love.

Here is a little of what the Bible has to say about the fear of the Lord: "The fear of the LORD is clean, enduring forever"

(Psalm 19:9). "The fear of the LORD is the beginning of wisdom, and the knowledge of the Holy One is understanding" (Proverbs 9:10). "The fear of the LORD is a fountain of life, to turn one away from the snares of death" (Proverbs 14:27).

When we begin to get a revelation of the fear of the Lord through being in His presence, the byproduct is understanding His amazing love, which never fails or fades, causing us to know that He is good. He is not surprised by our sin or shortcomings, but grieved when we do not respond to the loving sacrifice of His one and only Son.

That is where the enemy works overtime in our lives. He wants to push us face down into the dirt. But God's love lifts us up. He wants to remove the dirt and help us understand that He is good. The dirt—the sin—does not need to define us anymore. It is God's love that defines us and sets us free.

I want to love God more, because I know that, regardless of the waves of tribulation and testing that come, He continues to love me. Testing always produces a testimony. So embrace His love in the testings, because God wants to make such a testimony of your life that when you speak, you cause demons to flee out of others around you. That is why David could say, right in the midst of enemies closing in on him to eat him up, "The LORD is my light and my salvation" (Psalm 27:1 NIV). David did not care about the noise and clamor of the enemy. He wanted only to recalibrate his heart and "gaze on the beauty of the LORD" (verse 4).

Like David, you have a real enemy who hates you. He sounds like a lion, but he really is not. He is a liar and a thief. God wants to lift you above your enemy and set your feet on the Rock, who is Jesus. That is your rightful place as a son or daughter of the Most High God. When you are sitting with Him in heavenly places in Christ Jesus, your perspective changes, because then you see from His vantage point.

Face to Face with God

As the Israelites meandered in the wilderness for forty years, they were led by the smoky glory cloud by day and the pillar of fire by night. When the cloud or pillar moved, they would pack up and follow. They did not want to be left behind. And when the cloud or pillar stopped, they would establish camp again, each tribe situated in its place, and set everything up in the Tabernacle. Then Moses would go and meet the Lord, commune with Him, and receive the love, wisdom, and strength to lead the nation.

More than anything else, however, it was about a relationship. Moses had sweet intimacy speaking face to face with His Creator. The word *face* in Hebrew can also be translated *presence*. And we read in Numbers 12:8 (NASB) that God said of Moses, "With him I speak mouth to mouth." That is the literal Hebrew of how God and Moses spoke—mouth to mouth, breath to breath, presence to presence.

We are all invited to the place of face to face, presence to presence, where we have honest-to-goodness FaceTime with the God of the universe! That is where transformation comes and we become more like Him, rooted in His love, awakened to do great and mighty things. God wants to do that with us every day—breathe the breath of life, the breath of love, the breath of heaven—because we were created to live in His presence every day.

You may have read about the incredible minister and friend of God named Smith Wigglesworth, a powerful man in the Lord.

He spent hours and hours in God's presence, just listening and feeding himself with the Word of God. It was said that he would invite his ministry friends to spend time with him, praying and seeking the Lord's face. Friends who joined him in prayer said he would seem to leave himself and enter a different realm in his sincere communion with the Lord.

One day a pastor asked if he could spend time in prayer with Smith. Wigglesworth agreed and invited him into his prayer chamber. After some time, the weighty presence of the Lord so increased that the pastor, unable to stay any longer, crawled out, sobbing and broken. He said later that there was too much of God in that room, as the weighty glory of God had gotten heavier and heavier.

Through intimacy with God, Wigglesworth was able to remain in the glory longer than his friends.

The truth is, we were created to live in God's presence and bring Him glory, as David penned in Psalm 16:11: "In Your presence is fullness of joy." We must hunger and thirst for His presence. We must be after God's heart, after His face, and after His glory—because as we are touched with God's presence, it changes everything. It is from His presence that our lifestyle flows, and we become representations of Him.

Journey into Perfect Love

Say this prayer of declaration:

I am made for God's presence. I attract the very face of Almighty God, the very Presence Himself. I was made to have face time with God and behold His beauty, and as

I do, His wraparound presence protects and shields me. There is nothing that can separate me from the fire of perfect love. As I choose His presence and abide in all that He is, I will be overwhelmed and overcome by who He is in my life and who He has created me to be. I declare that I am bold and confident and overflowing with joy as I make room for His presence. Holy Spirit, let the fire of perfect love cascade over me and set me free to be who God has created me to be.

EIGHT

Grace to Embrace the Flame

"But we all, with unveiled face, beholding as in a mirror the glory of the Lord, are being transformed into the same image from glory to glory, just as by the Spirit of the Lord."

2 Corinthians 3:18

Rene

Have you ever sought God about something and actually found the answer by living it out? Holy Spirit often reveals things that have a big impact on our lives through the still, small voice of our everyday, ordinary activities. This was one of those times for me.

I was scheduled to speak at a conference on God's perspective on beauty. My cousin, who was hosting the event, was on her way to my house to plan and pray. Caught up in a phone call, I lost track of time and suddenly realized she would be arriving soon. My living room, where we would be meeting, was a mess and needed immediate attention. So I began rushing around, picking things up frantically and throwing them into my bedroom. Then I closed the door behind me.

At least I thought I closed it.

My cousin arrived and needed to use the restroom, which was right next to the bedroom. I watched her walk down the hallway, past the closed bathroom door and toward our bedroom door—which I saw was not closed but partially open. Horrified, I rushed down the hall after her as a voice in my head cried, *Nnnooo!* I tried to intercept her in what felt like a slow-motion moment, actually sticking my arm out to try to hold her back. It was too late.

My cousin went through the bedroom door, looked around, and said in a sincere voice, "Wow, your room is beautiful!"

Surprised, I replied, "It is?"

Then I noticed she was not looking at the mess, but at the rest of the room, which we had recently redecorated.

"Yes, I guess it is," I replied. "I mean—thank you very much!"

And then, slightly embarrassed, I escorted her out of the bedroom.

After my cousin found the room she was looking for, we met and prayed together about the conference.

After she left, I went back into the bedroom to start picking up the mess, slightly irritated and overwhelmed by it. Then I heard my cousin's words echo in my mind: *Wow, your room is beautiful!* This redirected my focus to look past the mess at the beauty of my room. I began to agree: *My room really is beautiful!*

I continued to gaze around the room as I picked up the mess, no longer irritated. I kept thinking, *I really do have a beautiful room!*—and a special grace came over me. I was not ignoring the mess, but now celebrating the beauty of the room, which empowered me to take care of the mess.

Radiating the Glory of God

In the same way that I saw my bedroom with fresh perspective, I believe it serves as a stunning parable in understanding the process of transformation from God's perspective. As we focus on the beauty of what Jesus has established in us through His extraordinary sacrifice, we are empowered to clean up what hinders the expression of His beauty in us.

The fire of perfect love burns inside every born-again believer. When we understand the grace-filled process of personal transformation, we can better cooperate with the fire of perfect love in transforming us from the inside out. As Paul writes,

> We all, with unveiled face, beholding as in a mirror the glory of the Lord, are being transformed into the same image from glory to glory, just as by the Spirit of the Lord.
>
> 2 Corinthians 3:18

His beauty becomes our beauty, and as we gaze upon it, we are transformed from glory to glory. We were made to radiate the beauty and glory of Jesus from the inside out. Our beauty is unveiled as we become a living expression of Isaiah 60:1 as "the glory of the Lord is risen upon you."

In a darkened world, we will appear as shining lights in the universe, guiding people to the One who is eternal life. Jesus, our majestic King, is seated at the right hand of the Father, interceding for us to come into the fullness of our love union with Him. Holy Spirit now resides on the inside of us, declaring, "Be holy, as I am holy." How does it happen? Only when we yield to the grace-filled, passionate fire of perfect love do we become the radiance of Christ on the earth.

In this chapter, I (Rene) will lay out the process of transformation with foundational truths and vivid imagery to help equip you, but it will take both courage and resolve for you to embrace the flame of perfect love in a way that consumes your entire being and transforms you into the image of Christ. You can actually become one heart and one flame with the God of all heaven and earth!

What I am sharing with you, I have been living out for twenty-five years, resulting in great personal freedom and transformation. When it is utilized as a powerful discipleship tool, I have seen it transform people from all different backgrounds—from those who have grown up in church, to successful lawyers and business owners, to those newly saved out of the occult—all with incredible testimonies of transformation.

Embracing the flame is part of my life message and a fulfillment of the prophetic promise I received when God invited me to lay down my modeling agency, with the promise that if I let it go, I would become an ambassador of His beauty.

Two Essentials for Transformation

As I have said, we must cooperate with God's Spirit and embrace the flame of perfect love. To understand how, we begin with a right understanding of two essentials, grace and the fear of the Lord, which are vitally important in our transformation process.

Grace

Grace is defined as unmerited favor and divine empowerment to overcome. The way we view God's heart toward us in our own sin and weakness determines whether we run *to*

God or *from* God. Grace brings a sense of confident assurance that God loves and enjoys us, even in our weakness. He loves us enough to not let us remain in our sin, and He gives us His divine empowerment to overcome. Father God rejoices in forgiving and restoring us. His grace empowers us to live in holiness, experiencing all that delights His heart.

In receiving God's love and forgiveness, we must be careful to not take His grace for granted, neither viewing it as something we are entitled to nor something we must earn. Trying produces striving. Relying on God's grace produces thriving.

All believers face times when we think we are strong in areas where we are actually weak. We become aware of a weakness that is new to us—but it is not new to God. It helps to understand that God sees the willing spirit of a sincere believer, even in the midst of weakness. When intense situations come and fear overtakes us, we realize that our flesh is weak. But God declares over us, "I see the *yes* and the *want to* of your willing spirit to do what is right, and it ravishes My heart!"

We see examples of this in Jesus' interactions with His disciples. He told Peter he would deny Him, for example, which Peter sincerely thought would never happen, but Jesus wanted him to know so that later he would pray and ask for help. After Peter's denial, when he went back to his old life of fishing out of shame, the resurrected Jesus came to him and spoke to what He knew was in Peter's heart—his weak but sincere love—and Peter was restored.

The only way the enemy wins in our lives is when we give up by not receiving God's grace in our failure. Let's not underestimate the amazing grace we can receive from God when we discover something we did not know was inside us, when we choose to be brave enough to face it, and when we pray for help to overcome it. Even our weak love moves the heart of God.

The Fear of the Lord

The fear of the Lord can be defined as an attitude of respect, admiration, and love for God with a profound reverence for and awe of His power. Fear of the Lord declares that He is the supreme power over all, and that we are humbled in light of it. The fear of the Lord helps us identify other lovers or idols in our lives that try to divide our hearts and hinder our union with Him.

The fear of the Lord strengthens us in confidence to embrace His mercy, knowing that Almighty God is on our side, and it frees us from fearing others and their opinions. When we live in obedient devotion to God, the fear of the Lord truly is the beginning of wisdom and knowledge (see Proverbs 9:10).

The Essentials in Balance

Grace and the fear of the Lord are like two sides of the same coin. If you want to live fully in grace, you must live fully in the fear of the Lord. If you receive grace without fear of the Lord, you will live a compromised and entitled life: "I can live any way I want; it doesn't matter. God loves me and forgives me anyway." You will remain in your weakness rather than be empowered to overcome and be set apart. And Paul writes, "Shall we continue in sin that grace may abound? Certainly not!" (Romans 6:1–2).

If, on the other hand, you fear the Lord without grace, you will fall under the judgment of law and good works. You will feel condemned, rejected, unworthy, insignificant, never good enough.

The fear of the Lord and grace operate with equal importance in the transformation process of our lives. From a yielded place of humility, we acknowledge the magnitude of God's greatness, seeing how small we really are, and we also accept His invitation to rise up into His greatness, never forgetting from whom that greatness comes. We go low in reverent awe and receive empowerment to be raised up. Jesus did not stay on the cross, and neither should we; however, neither did He bypass the cross, and we are to pick ours up daily.

We need to embrace both the intensity of the fear of the Lord and the confident assurance of grace that empowers us to live in holiness, experiencing all that delights God's heart.

> Beloved friends, what should be our proper response to God's marvelous mercies? To surrender yourselves to God to be his sacred, living sacrifices. And live in holiness, experiencing all that delights His heart. For this becomes your genuine expression of worship.
>
> Romans 12:1 TPT

The Transformation Process

The Bible teaches that humans are made of three parts—spirit, soul, and body (see 1 Thessalonians 5:23). We were created in the image of God as tripartite beings, three in one, just as God is three in one. Each part of us is distinct in role and function, yet interconnected and influencing each other part, while we operate as one.

Here are brief descriptions of each part:

- **Spirit.** The innermost part of a person—we might call it the heart—connects and communicates with God and perceives the spiritual realm (see John 3:6;

Romans 8:16). The spirit is the life force, wind, or breath.

- **Soul.** The soul, our inner nature, is composed of our *mind*, *will*, and *emotions*. The soul perceives things in the psychological realm and is what gives us personality (see Psalm 103:1–5; 146:1–2).

- **Body.** The physical body (see Psalm 139:13–16) is, for the believer, the temple of Holy Spirit (see 1 Corinthians 3:16; 6:19), and is the external part of us that makes tangible contact with the world using five physical senses: sight, hearing, taste, smell, and touch. Our senses are gateways to our soul.

This diagram illustrates the three parts together in a circular pattern. The body is the outward, physical part that houses the

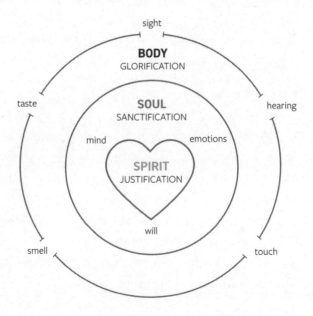

soul; the soul is the inward part that houses the spirit; and the spirit is the innermost, hidden part that connects with God. Three Christian terms describe the work of transformation that takes place in each of these parts, from the inside out—*justification, sanctification,* and *glorification*—effecting the process of salvation from new birth to resurrection. It is important to identify what God's role is in the process, and what ours is.

- **Justification.** We are justified—"just-as-if-we-never-sinned"—in our spirits. Justification is all about what God's love did for us through the one-time perfect sacrifice of Jesus on the cross. There is absolutely nothing we could ever do to earn or deserve salvation. We simply choose to believe and receive it as a gift. Once we do, God sees us through the finished work of the cross—righteous, flawless, and holy. We are new creations with a new nature. Justification is an act of God on our behalf, freeing us from the penalty of sin. We are "justified freely by His grace through the redemption that is in Christ Jesus" (Romans 3:24).

- **Sanctification.** Sanctification is the process that takes place in the soul, in which we cooperate with Holy Spirit to grow in holiness, living a set-apart life. This is our response to what God's love did for us. Through justification, the *penalty* of sin is broken off our lives, and through sanctification, the *power* of sin is broken. This takes place progressively in our everyday walk in the Spirit as we yield freely to His power and refuse to gratify the desires of the flesh. Sanctification is the process of growth in spiritual maturity in which the *mind* is renewed, the *will* is yielded, and the *emotions* are healed. "Now I commit you to God and to the word of his grace, which can build you up and give you an inheritance among all those who are sanctified" (Acts 20:32 NIV).

- **Glorification.** This is the manifestation of God's glory in the physical body—the outward manifestation of an internal reality. How much glory we radiate in our physical bodies on earth is determined by our cooperation with Holy Spirit in being transformed into the image of Jesus Christ (see 2 Thessalonians 1:12). The fullness of this manifestation happens when we are resurrected into eternal life (see 1 Corinthians 15:42–44).

These three works of transformation working together can be summarized like this: We are born again in Christ and made righteous in God's sight, forever justified (justification); we are being sanctified as we grow in holiness through Holy Spirit (sanctification); and we display a measure of God's glory in our lives while on earth, and fully when resurrected into eternal life (glorification). If we try to achieve these works in our own strength or power, we will fail. What began in the Spirit must continue by the Spirit. We need to receive God's grace continually through faith, and rely on the power of His Spirit to transform us from the inside out.

The Power Source

I pray that he would unveil within you the unlimited riches of his glory and favor until supernatural strength floods your innermost being with his divine might and explosive power.

Ephesians 3:16 TPT

Holy Spirit is the life-giving power source who helps us access all the glorious riches of Christ Jesus. We receive the gift of God's Spirit at conversion, by whom we are sealed for the day of redemption, and He takes up residence in our spirits.

John the Baptist said that Jesus baptized with water for repentance, but that after him would come One more powerful, Jesus, who would baptize "with the Holy Spirit and fire" (Matthew 3:11). God's eternal living flame of love is deposited in the very core of our innermost being. Then the fire of God's perfect love burns on the altar of our hearts, perfecting us from the inside out. Holy Spirit's job description is found in His name: *Holy!* He helps us grow in holiness.

Imagine that the power source gift of Holy Spirit is like a grenade dropped inside of us. The baptism of Holy Spirit and fire is like the pin of the grenade being pulled, releasing the source of that power. We are continually being filled with this power through our cooperation in the sanctification process as the unlimited riches of Christ's glory are unveiled within us.

The living flame of love that has been ignited within us desires to fill our entire being. The passion of Christ consumes us as His glorious riches are displayed through us. His burning desire is to fill each part of our souls—mind, will, and emotions—and burn up anything that hinders God's perfect love. We must learn not to grieve or quench the work of Holy Spirit in our lives (see Ephesians 4:30). This is what it means to work out the fullness of salvation (spirit, soul, body) with fear and trembling as described in Philippians 2:12.

God's refining fire brings impurities to the surface, not to condemn us but to reveal the glory inside of us. When gold is refined, the heat brings the dross to the surface to be scraped off, revealing the purity of the gold. When we understand that

God's intent is to bring out the best version of who we are, we can yield more easily to His work in us and trust the process of restoration.

The Garden and the Sword

The Garden of Eden provides a stunning parallel to the transformation process in our hearts. Let's look at what God put into place in the Garden of Eden after the Fall, what Jesus did to restore us, and how Holy Spirit is now at work in our hearts.

What did God put into place in the Garden of Eden as a result of the Fall?

> The LORD God said, "Behold, the man has become like one of Us, to know good and evil. And now, lest he put out his hand and take also of the tree of life, and eat, and live forever"—therefore the LORD God sent him out of the garden of Eden to till the ground from which he was taken. So He drove out the man; and He placed cherubim at the east of the garden of Eden, and a flaming sword which turned every way, to guard the way to the tree of life.
>
> Genesis 3:22–24

By placing cherubim and a flaming sword to guard the Tree of Life after the Fall, Father God protected Adam and Eve from eating of that Tree and living forever in their fallen state.

Then, through the resurrection power of Jesus Christ, God provided a way for mankind to return to the garden of His delight. Rather than remain in our sins, we can now live in Jesus Christ, "the way, the truth, and the life" (John 14:6). Jesus hung on a tree (the cross) to become the *way* back to the Tree of Life. He was resurrected from a garden tomb to restore us to a relationship with Father God.

When Jesus baptizes us with Holy Spirit and fire (as we saw in Matthew 3:11), the flaming sword of truth sealed in our spirits flashes back and forth over our souls, offering life-giving *truth* and restoration. The flaming sword divides flesh from spirit and truth from lies. It wages war on demonic strongholds and brings an end to their rule, as we cooperate with God in taking back the dominion of our souls.

His fire burns up what hinders love, and His grace empowers us to choose to walk the narrow path.

Every part of the soul is now given the opportunity to taste and see that the Lord is good. We can eat freely of the Tree of Life through the resurrection power of Christ, making our way back to abundant life. Jesus' radical obedience to death and subsequent resurrection freed us from the curse of sin, and with every act of our obedience, we are freed from the effect of sin in our souls. Every obedient choice we make to eat from the Tree of Life allows its branches to grow and spread out in our souls, manifesting the fruit of the Spirit in our lives. And this fruit draws others to taste its redemption. "To the one who overcomes, I will grant to eat from the tree of life, which is in the Paradise of God" (Revelation 2:7 NASB).

From Genesis to Revelation, humanity is offered the fullness of restoration as we come full circle back to the Garden—back to an abundant life. God's heart is that we would flourish in the garden of His delight.

Renewing, Yielding, Healing

How is it that Holy Spirit, who is called the Comforter, moves in ways we are not always comfortable with? When He wages war against our flesh (see Galatians 5:17), this makes our flesh very uncomfortable. When the flame of first love goes after idols in our soul, Holy Spirit does not comfort our flesh but brings us into the intensity of the fire.

The things of the Spirit always offend the flesh. To function in the supernatural power of God, we must embrace childlike faith and command our souls to take a back seat and align with the Spirit of God within us and the greater reality of God's Kingdom. Our old, selfish nature needs to give way to our new nature, our new mind, our new thoughts, our new emotions. Then Holy Spirit will help us to find comfort in embracing His flame, rather than running from it to find comfort in other, lesser lovers.

When self-pity raises its whiny head, we need to wave the white flag of surrender over it, raise up the victory flag, and proclaim, "I can do all things through Christ who strengthens me" (Philippians 4:13). When we pick up our cross daily and crucify the old self, we make room for more of God's life-giving Spirit. The more crucified we are, the more full of Him we are! We get the way better end of the deal, gaining so much more than we give up. (You may need to remind your soul of that when it is kicking and screaming for its way.) The old nature is done away with, and the new has come.

Our unredeemed, selfish desires want revenge. They want to hang on to offense. They are guarded, divided. They use distorted love to control and manipulate. They are conditional; they want their own way; they have self-seeking motives.

Holy Spirit, on the other hand, always leads us to love through forgiveness, releasing offense, invitation, reconciliation, speaking truth, preferring others, serving, giving love freely and uncon-ditionally, considering our ways, having pure motives. He leads us to the will of the Father—all saved, all healed, all delivered.

Let's look at each aspect of the soul as it cooperates with the transforming work of God's Spirit.

Renewing the Mind

Holy Spirit is at work renewing our minds, so we have the same attitude Jesus had.

> Do not conform to the pattern of this world, but be transformed by the renewing of your mind. Then you will be able to test and approve what God's will is—his good, pleasing and perfect will.
>
> Romans 12:2 NIV

God wants us to take every thought captive to obey Christ, and to trust in Him completely and not rely on our own opinions, so that His peace, which surpasses all understanding, will guard our hearts and minds.

The intellect is a beautiful gift from God, but often it tries to be "control central." If not kept in check, it will even use spiritual head knowledge from God's Word, the Bible, to validate its superiority over the Spirit of God, who wishes to be seated on the throne of our hearts.

Instead, in order to nurture radical, childlike faith and trust, we need to wage war on doublemindedness and subdue it. A discerning mind—but not a suspicious mind!—is greatly needed in the Church. When the Spirit of God leads our intellect, we can operate in pure discernment.

Yielding the Will

To come into the fullness of what the fire of perfect love will produce in us, we must be about our Father's business and yield our wills to Father God, just as Jesus did. Holy Spirit knows the perfect will of our Father and always leads us to it.

Our choice to submit is vital. Unfortunately, with a history of harsh religious application, the word *submit* carries negative connotations. But a definition of the word as translated from the Aramaic reveals that *to submit* means "to tenderly devote oneself." To say that I devote myself tenderly to God or to my husband captures the beauty of what it means to submit.

God has given us free will to choose. In His goodness, once we choose to put our faith in Jesus Christ as Savior, we are forever justified. And then we are being sanctified continually through our everyday choices in yielding to His direction. His way is the right way even when we do not understand it. Whenever I begin to doubt the goodness of God's leadership, Holy Spirit reminds me of the love Jesus displayed on the cross, which declared, "This is how much I love you." What more could God do to prove His love for us? His love is perfect and so is His direction.

As we follow God's desires, He leads us along narrow paths. They are not easy, but as we yield our desires to Him, something beautiful happens. Soon we find ourselves coming through the narrow way into wide open spaces where God gives us the desires of our hearts, because His desires have become our desires.

Yielding the will requires the beauty of repentance, which is simply turning from what is not of God to that which is of God—from lies to truth, from thoughts and ways that are not God's to thoughts and ways that are. When we react to situations in our fleshly emotions rather than responding to God's Spirit, we repent. Being unteachable can be the result of not understanding how much God enjoys us in our messy process. It can also come from perceiving repentance according to the harshness of religion, rather than with the ease and tenderness of our Father inviting us into what is good for us. Yielding allows us to be teachable and to grow in maturity.

Healing the Emotions

Our emotions are a beautiful gift from God, part of being made in His image. God is not emotionless, and neither should His glorious Church be. God desires, weeps, laughs, shows compassion, expresses righteous anger, and rejoices over us with singing (to name just a few). But in our efforts to prevent emotion from leading us, the Church has gone to the extreme of becoming passionless and shut down. When we receive the revelation that Jesus was first passionate for us, on the other hand, we come alive and become passionate for Him.

Just as we do not shut down our minds, but submit them to the Spirit of God's leading, so is it with our emotions. They are not to be shut down, but rather submitted to the Lord. God wants our emotions to be fully alive in Him and for us to experience His love deeply.

Tremendous healing is needed in the emotional makeup of the Church. A whole generation has much pain on display, manifesting itself in rage, suicide, self-mutilation, broken relationships, eating disorders, and addictions, to name only a few. We said in the last chapter that the Lord showed us, through our daughter's difficult birth, many parallels to what others in her generation have faced, and what the redemptive purposes and plans of the Lord are for them. Nothing can heal this generation more deeply than the healing touch of God's perfect love.

Setting a Guard

It is important in our transformation process to set a guard over the gateways of our five senses (eyes, ears, nose, mouth, touch), and to watch what we allow in and what is coming out. Solomon wrote, "Above all else, guard your heart, for everything you do flows from it" (Proverbs 4:23 NIV).

What you allow through the gateways of your five senses really matters. It affects your entire being—spirit, soul, body. What you listen to is what you put your faith in. When you receive life-giving words, they build faith in your spirit, which weakens and puts to death your selfish, sinful desires. "Faith comes by hearing, and hearing by the word of God" (Romans 10:17). When you build up your spirit, God's voice is the loudest in your life, and the loudest voice wins!

Is your faith in God's Word or in the voices of the world? Are you listening for the report of the Lord or to worldly reports? God wants you to lean into His heart and listen for what He is speaking over your life, into your personal situation, and into world affairs. May your spiritual ears be fully awakened and alert to hear how the Spirit of God is leading you into all truth and restoration.

We are familiar with how various foods coming into our bodies through our mouths affect us. When we eat food that is bad for us, it affects our physical health. The principle of "we are what we eat" also holds true in the spiritual realm. If we allow toxic words or images to feed the appetite of the beast—our own selfish desires—then we will act beastly. On the other hand, when we feast our ears and eyes on what is pure, lovely, and of good report, we become the beautiful radiance of Christ on the earth.

So which will it be, beauty or the beast?

What we see, hear, and act on through our five sensory gateways are often indicators of inward reality, and they are helpful in letting us know what needs attention. When these manifestations come to the surface, rather than ignore them or hide in shame, we can embrace the grace and empowerment to take action. Holy Spirit will bring us awareness and help us to repent and ask forgiveness when we blow it and react from our flesh, and celebrate when we respond in a godly way.

Poor health resulting from bad eating habits can stem from an emotional need in the soul for comfort. Someone needing peace and calm may find a false sense of it in a drug, while Jesus wants to give us His genuine peace and calm. Learning to forgive and love oneself also becomes important in the healing process.

Whenever things come to the surface, simply come out of agreement with whatever is offering a temporary fix for your need. Repent and agree with what God says, and ask Him to fill that need with His love and truth.

Receiving God's Perfect Love

Rene

Before receiving Christ, I lived a promiscuous life. I had some understanding of how that could affect me physically, but I did not understand the driving forces behind it—the need of the little girl in my soul to know she was beautiful and valuable, and the spiritual strongholds hooked into my soul from my own choices and the choices made by others in generations past.

After I gave my heart to Jesus, Holy Spirit helped me understand that what I allowed through the sexual gateway, the gateway of touch, affected my entire being deeply. When I engaged in intercourse outside of marriage, I was also sleeping with every person that person had slept with, not only physically but spiritually, resulting in soul ties, unholy blood covenants, and seducing spirits.

At first the realization of these connections overwhelmed me, but then God overwhelmed me with His beautiful grace and love. He led me to write down every person's name, and then take red paint and apply it over the piece of paper, symbolizing the blood of Jesus covering those sins and breaking their power over me. I renounced and repented as God's Spirit spoke to me about my worth and began the process of cleansing.

Later I received more healing in my emotions as the realization came to the surface that I still yearned to be desired by men. I cried out, "God, I want the desire to be beautiful to You and to my husband to be enough. Please take away this need to be desired by other men."

I kept praying this until, over time, freedom came. Holy Spirit continued to heal my emotions and deliver me from a seducing spirit by the fire of His perfect love. It was not a big deliverance—more like a gentle surgeon unraveling an unclean spirit from my identity. My emotions started receiving God's beautiful desire for me, and His pure beauty began manifesting itself in my life. That other desire was completely gone.

Just as physical wounds need healing, so do wounds in the soul—the mind, will, and emotions. We can put bandages over those areas, trying to cover them up, but the wounds are still festering, and a demonic stronghold can settle under the bandages like an infection. This is how sincere believers in Jesus, sealed with Holy Spirit in their spirits, can have demonic strongholds in their souls from which they need deliverance. Holy

Spirit lifts off each bandage compassionately, cleans out the infection—the demonic stronghold—and applies His healing balm of truth and love.

So let's feast our senses on receiving pure and perfect love from God, and put boundaries in our lives for what comes in and out of the gateways of our senses. Let's establish in our hearts and homes a culture of what is pure and lovely as fuel for the fire of His perfect love.

The Glorious Renovation

Holy Spirit wants to renovate your entire being, in the same way you might renovate your home.

When you put your faith in Jesus Christ for salvation, you invited Holy Spirit into your living room. He is now the general contractor (GC) of your spirit, who manages and collaborates with you throughout the transformation process, all the way through the soul of our home's completion. He is highly qualified, with rock-solid references and timeless experience, and He works with the Father's heavenly blueprints to restore you to the historic beauty of your original design.

He sees the completed work and beauty of the whole house and enjoys the renovation process, including setting inspections and shining a light on what needs attention. He handles the demolition of walls of self-protection, if needed, and He does a great job managing waste disposal, getting rid of sin. He never loses sight of the completed project and celebrates even when it gets messy. Our GC shares His renovation plans with us continually for agreement, and He surveys the foundations of our faith in order to strengthen any compromised areas.

He is patient with us in the process and goes where He is invited throughout the house of our souls. He goes from level to level, room to room, desiring to work with the subcontractors of our souls—the mind, the will, and the emotions. The more these subcontractors cooperate with Him, the more smoothly the project goes.

He remodels our lives by revealing the truth and renewing our *minds*. He restores desolate places of pain and brokenness to heal our *emotions*. How much renovation our GC does depends on our *wills*—how we cooperate with Him in the process.

He points to areas that need fixing, not to condemn the house but to transform it into the fullness of its intended beauty. And He identifies any unwanted squatters He finds in the house—those demonic strongholds—and serves and enforces eviction notices.

Remember, Holy Spirit sees everything in your life through the lens of love and enjoys working with you. He loves your honest questions and your sincere process. Even your weak and stubborn moments He can handle. He especially loves those moments when you start to get a clue as more skylights are added to the house, shedding light on the process!

You will never find a more committed friend than the Friend you have in Holy Spirit, who will continually lead you into all truth. He is graciously at work, bringing forth the best version of you.

"'This Temple is going to end up far better than it started out, a glorious beginning but an even more glorious finish: a place in which I will hand out wholeness and holiness.' Decree of God-of-the-Angel-Armies."

Haggai 2:9 MSG

Journey into Perfect Love

Holy Spirit is excited to complete the work He has begun in your life! He enjoys the process of restoration. As you cooperate with Him in the restoration process, remember that He sees the beauty of the completed work, and wants you to see it, too. Your life really is beautiful!

- Ask Holy Spirit to reveal the beauty of who you are according to your original design and the abundant life He has for you.
- Invite the fire of His perfect love to burn up things in your soul that hinder love, and thank Him for revealing the glory of your original design. Let Him know you want to come out of agreement with thoughts or emotions that are untrue, unhealthy, or contrary to His life-giving Spirit.
- Ask Holy Spirit if there are any walls that need to come down in your soul. If so, you can invite Him to do the demolition in order to open up room to receive more of His love and restoration.
- As for those unwanted squatters (demonic strongholds), ask Holy Spirit if you need to extend forgiveness, or if there is a lie you are believing, so the squatter has no legal right to be there. Once that is done, tell those unwelcome intruders you want them out of your soul. Tell them they no longer have any legal right to you, and ask Holy Spirit to serve an eviction notice sealed with the blood of Jesus. Then ask Holy Spirit to fill the emptied space with His goodness and glory and to continue to fill your whole house with His glory.

NINE

Burning Hotter than Persecution

"Look!" he answered, "I see four men loose, walking in the midst of the fire; and they are not hurt, and the form of the fourth is like the Son of God."

Daniel 3:25

We have had the privilege of ministering in many nations throughout the earth, and have been sent into very dark places spiritually. Time and again we have seen that the darker the place, the greater the release of God's power, with incredible healings and deliverances. When the fire of perfect love blazes inside us, dark spiritual powers have to bow to the resurrected King. We walk in authority not only over darkness, but in the power to love those who persecute us. The fire of love helps us separate the spiritual darkness at work from the person whom God made in His image.

Persecution is to be expected when you are on mission to set captives free. We, Steven and Rene, have faced both physical and spiritual attacks. We have had guns pulled on us; we have been beaten; we have been chased through streets by religious leaders with rocks in their hands wanting to stone us (yes, Old Testament style); and we have faced attacks in the night, both physical and demonic, from the curses of witch doctors. Once we led a gang member to the Lord in our living room and later found a knife in our couch, left there after the man dropped to his knees in repentance.

Our base in Ghana is located in the area in West Africa where voodoo originated, and we have had several direct assaults from witch doctors, both physical and spiritual. We have had head-to-head confrontations and incantations being said over us while we were releasing God's healing power and watching paralyzed people walking, eyes being opened, and large facial tumors dissolving and crumbling off. And we have witnessed witch doctors being saved, healed, and delivered.

After one former witch doctor gave her life to Jesus, we went to clean out her hut to get rid of all the things that had been used in rituals and incantations. We were ready for an intense spiritual battle. Instead, when the village people gathered to watch what was happening, the power of God restored the physical sight of that former witch doctor, who had been blind. Revival broke out in the wonder of it all, resulting in salvation and healing for all who gathered to watch. We baptized the former witch doctor the next day in the river.

Darkness must bow to the power of perfect love burning in us. As we stand as God's sons and daughters in the power and authority of Jesus Christ, the fire of perfect love consumes spiritual darkness.

Sometimes the hardest persecution comes from those in the Church. This was hard for us at first when we were young, sincere believers, lacking wisdom and having a lot to learn about what to share and with whom. We did not expect opposition to come from within. But as we burn hot in the flame of love, it causes many things to flare up around us, especially a religious spirit. It is difficult to be misunderstood by leaders, or persecuted in words from the pulpit. It is tough to stand on the spiritual frontlines with comrades who later turn on you.

We have learned to forgive people who (as Jesus said on the cross) do not know what they are doing. But we have also had great times of reconciliation with those same people, and we enjoy deep, rich, lifelong covenant relationships that stand the test of time and conflict.

And as we remain teachable, there are things about leadership that we appreciate more, now that we walk in those shoes and have greater understanding of the intense pressure leaders have to learn to release to the Lord.

We do and say things in the midst of pressure unlike how we act most of the time. And sometimes people remember that one time and forget all the rest. But there is no place in our souls to harbor offenses—which we have talked about already, and which is one of the most crippling problems in the Body of Christ, both emotionally and spiritually. Jesus carried the sins of the world on Himself on the cross, so let's let our offenses die there, too. God's grace is available to release offenses to be burned up in the fire of perfect love.

Colliding Kingdoms

Rene

I am not confrontational by nature. But although I prefer a gentler approach, that is not always what is needed. Conflict can be a great opportunity for us to co-labor with God. Steven is bold and does not shy away from confrontation. But he has learned when a gentler approach is needed—for example, in our marriage.

As the fire of perfect love burns hotter in me than my fear of conflict, a Holy Spirit boldness comes on me, along with an authority to bring the Kingdom of heaven to earth. I have been in awe of some wonderful things I have gotten to co-labor with God for, when His love burns hotter than fear.

Steven

I recall one time, at the end of one of our trips to Ghana, we had concluded our time of ministry at the Transformation Center and were staying at a hotel near the coast before returning to the U.S. Rene and I, along with another couple, were walking along the beach when we were stopped by a muscular and aggressive young man. He demanded money from the four of us and began to talk about his god.

"Which god are you talking about?" I asked.

"The god of the sea, the fish god."

"Huh," I said. "That's interesting. We worship the uncreated God who created all the things you see before you."

He replied that that was his beach, his domain, and we had to pay him money.

"No," I said. "Actually, the earth is the Lord's and everything that's in it. I won't pay you money, but we will pray for you."

He refused prayer and began to press in toward us, trying to threaten and intimidate the four of us. But we stood our ground, praying in the Spirit under our breath, and even aloud at times.

"You will pay me," he said. "We will see to it that you pay me."

Then he pointed to his friends, up along the shelter wall on the beach, who started to advance toward us.

"We will pay you nothing," I repeated. "Again, the earth is the Lord's. It belongs to the uncreated God, the One we love and serve. By the way, if you look behind you, you won't like what you see, and neither will the demons you serve. There is a myriad of angels standing guard, and they will protect us."

As soon as I said this, the young man and his demons seemed to become aware of the angelic presence. He stopped pressing us and stepped back reluctantly, and his friends stopped in their tracks. Then we turned around and walked back to our hotel.

The lesson in all this? We are always on a mission. The four of us may have been heading home, but the battle does not stop just because our mission trip is done. And in the face of persecution, we must cling to the Spirit of love, grace, and power—the hope of glory inside us. "You, dear children, are from God and have overcome [demonic spirits], because the one who is in you is greater than the one who is in the world" (1 John 4:4 NIV).

Into the Fire

The enemy is always spewing fear and wants us to be afraid, to intimidate us, to distract us from holding fast to who our Father says we are. So when all hell is against you, remember that all of heaven is for you. In the face of persecution and accusation, remember that, by divine design, you are a son or daughter of God. He will guard you; He will keep you.

> God sends angels with special orders to protect you wherever you go, defending you from all harm. If you walk into a trap, they'll be there for you and keep you from stumbling.
>
> Psalm 91:11–12 TPT

The Bible is full of images of fire, and "our God is a consuming fire" (Hebrews 12:29). He wants us to be full of fire, too, because His consuming, fiery love removes the hindrances that keep us from encountering the depths of His love.

Deuteronomy 4:24 (AMP): "The LORD your God is a consuming fire; He is a jealous (impassioned) God [demanding what is rightfully and uniquely His]." God's fire purifies. Jesus joins us in the fire. Jesus baptizes and immerses us with fire. Fire is His holy passion.

Exodus 24:17: "The sight of the glory of the LORD was like a consuming fire on the top of the mountain in the eyes of the children of Israel." God wants us to see Him as He really is.

When you think of consuming fire, think about God's unfailing and unhindered love. His love is fire in its purest and most honest sense. When He showed himself to Moses and the Israelites, He wanted them to see His glory and power. In effect, Moses ran into the fire of God's presence, while the Israelites turned back and asked Moses to go instead.

In this day and hour, God is inviting His people once again not only to the foot of the mountain, but up onto the mountain, to the place where His burning glory and fire purify and sanctify and overwhelm us with His love.

The three young Hebrew exiles in Babylon were threatened by fire when they refused to worship the massive gold statue King Nebuchadnezzar had set up. They held fast to their conviction that there is no god but the one true God. Purity and loving God will do this. And when King Nebuchadnezzar threatened to throw them into the blazing furnace, they stood their ground, unmoved by the threat.

Keep in mind, this was not a little oven in which you would bake your cake or heat your pot roast; it was a furnace used for smelting metal like gold or silver. It may have been used for baking bricks for construction. It was huge and hot, hot, hot!

Still they refused to bow before the gold statue. "We are bowing to the one true God," they said, "and that's it. Him alone."

This so enraged Nebuchadnezzar that he ordered the furnace heated up seven times hotter than usual. It was their standing strong for the Lord that got them thrown into the flames.

> Suddenly, Nebuchadnezzar jumped up in amazement and exclaimed to his advisers, "Didn't we tie up three men and throw them into the furnace?"
>
> "Yes, Your Majesty, we certainly did," they replied.
>
> "Look!" Nebuchadnezzar shouted. "I see four men, unbound, walking around in the fire unharmed! And the fourth looks like a god!"
>
> Then Nebuchadnezzar came as close as he could to the door of the flaming furnace and shouted: "Shadrach, Meshach, and Abednego, servants of the Most High God, come out! Come here!"
>
> So Shadrach, Meshach, and Abednego stepped out of the fire. Then the high officers, officials, governors, and advisers crowded around them and saw that the fire had not touched them. Not a hair on their heads was singed, and their clothing was not scorched. They didn't even smell of smoke!
>
> Daniel 3:24–27 NLT

Those three Jewish men were at peace as they walked around in the fire, witnesses for the Lord God Almighty. This created an incredible opportunity for God to show who He really is. As those three men stood their ground, God showed up in a miraculous way and joined them in the fire.

Because we know how the story goes. Suddenly there was a fourth Man in the furnace with Shadrach, Meshach, and Abednego, His fiery hedge surrounding them.

The only ones who were burned and died that day were the soldiers who threw the men in. The men in the fire lived—set free and joined by the King of kings. When they emerged, there were no ropes binding them (the NASB says they were "untied"), and they did not even smell like smoke. And Nebuchadnezzar was given the revelation that their God is the only God.

Once you have embraced the flame of God's love first and foremost, when flames of accusation come, you will be able to stand in peace as one who is more than a conqueror, knowing that God's love has conquered *you*. And when the enemy tries to catch you and put you in a snare, Jesus will join you in the fire.

So don't play around the fire; get into it. You are called to be a house of prayer—one of His burning ones who, when testings and persecutions come, does not quit. You do not run from the fire; you run into the fire, and God will join you there, because He is the fire. There is no better place to be than in the fire of God's love.

Shadrach, Meshach, and Abednego said, "If our God shows up, great!—and if He doesn't, it's still great because we will be with Him" (see Daniel 3:17–18). They had confidence. They were not going to bow to some foreign god or idol. Yet many of us in the Church are quick to lose our traction and focus and get pulled off course.

Often, after we pass the testings and trials by fire, promotion comes. Look what happened to the three Jewish men as they came out of the fiery furnace: "The king promoted Shadrach, Meshach, and Abednego to even higher positions in the province of Babylon" (Daniel 3:30). So be prepared for your promotion as you embrace the Man of fire.

A friend of mine is a military veteran. In his combat training, he was instructed that, when the enemy began to shoot, the best option was to run into the fire—the direction where the bullets were coming from. If he ran back to the left or to the right, the enemy fire was more certain to get him. But if he ran toward where the firing was coming from and closed the gap on the enemy, his chances of success would be much greater.

In the same way, as we navigate spiritual warfare, we are called not to retreat but to advance. So just run into the fire, because we have this shield called faith, which quenches every fiery dart of the enemy (see Ephesians 6:16)—and "without faith it is impossible to please God" (Hebrews 11:6 NIV). The enemy has his fire, but it is not all-consuming; it is just darts or noise. Our God is all-consuming; He joins us in the fire and even consumes the work of the enemy's fire. And when we are clothed in the full armor of God, with each article of armor in place (see Ephesians 6:11–18), we stand completely protected in Him. After all, it is His armor.

When warriors ran with locked shields, it created a clamshell of protection around them when fiery darts came. The Romans dipped their shields, which had leather exteriors, into water, and when flaming arrows came, the water put the fire out. Today the water is nothing more than being dipped in Holy Spirit, swimming with Him over our heads, so all His waves crash over us and immerse us, and the shield of faith quenches the fiery darts.

Standing Boldly

We work regularly with the persecuted Church around the world. Some of the stories of their endurance in the face of persecution are astounding.

One of our beloved pastors, motivated by the power of God's Word, has been attacked and beaten because of his heart of love. One day, as he shared the love of Jesus and fed the poor of the community, an angry mob approached with threats and derogatory slurs. As they closed in, one of the men had a hand behind his back, apparently holding something as he ran toward him. Our friend heard the voice of the Lord say, *Duck down.*

At that moment, as he ducked, the man threw a container at him. It was filled with acid. By ducking down, he avoided having his entire face doused with acid; but it still landed on part of his neck and back, burning his skin severely.

He was attacked just because he shared the fiery, passionate love of Jesus to a less fortunate group of people who were beloved by God and created in His image.

Steven

Over the years we have enjoyed taking teams on mission trips all over the planet. One time, as we took a team to Italy, the Lord gave us simple instructions to go worship and declare His goodness on the seven hills of Rome. And in each of those places, as we prayed and worshiped, we experienced divine encounters.

On one of the hills, it appeared that nobody was there. But as we began to worship and pray, several men started to drop out of the trees. It was shocking! Suddenly the hill was being filled with people, the sound of prayer and worship bringing them out of the trees. One by one, they came and stood around us as we worshiped and sang praises to God.

Who were these men? What were they doing in the trees?

One young man who spoke English told us that they were Kurdish refugees escaping the persecution they had come under in Northern Iraq. They were looking for a place of safety, a new place to call home, and were now living and sleeping in these trees.

As we continued to worship, we had an opportunity to pray for them and encourage them. Suddenly one of the men began to scream at us in Arabic. We did not understand him but could hear his vehemence. Another man translating for us relayed how much that man, who was Iraqi, hated Americans.

At first we were taken aback. We were there showing the love of God to these refugees and seeing Him touch hearts. But that man kept interrupting, full of anger and hatred. We could see it in his eyes. In fact, we thought maybe he was going to start throwing punches, so we were ready, even as we prayed in the Spirit.

Rene and part of the team remained in worship and prayer, while others of us began to interact with the man. Violence and tension filled the air.

I began to share with him that just because of one individual's actions or choices, or even because of the position of our government, he should not hate the whole country. And if his leader was evil and destroying Kurdish refugees, threatening even the men who were with us now, I said, "Should I hate you then, too? And should these men around you hate you?"

As we continued to talk, and the team continued to pray in the Spirit, the atmosphere began to shift, and God came with His peace. The man heard the words of love and compassion and began to soften. We ended up embracing each other. Although he was Muslim, he allowed us to pray for him; and the team had the opportunity to pray over this man the *shalom* of the uncreated God.

I could tell through his change of expression, body language, and tone of voice that the overwhelming love of the Father was coming on him, and that His descending love was touching this man's heart.

We in the Western Church have been isolated from much of the persecution happening to our brothers and sisters in other nations. But regardless of what we are going through, God wants us to find refuge in Him. He is our help in time of trouble, as we saw that day in Rome. We learn to hold fast in the middle of trial or danger, knowing that if God is for us, who can be against us? We stand with boldness and confidence in faith. God's presence was there, His angels were there, and His love was there, touching and changing a human heart.

Later, after this remarkable encounter, the group we were with on this mission started an outreach to Kurdish refugees coming through Rome, looking for a safe haven where they could raise their families without fear of being destroyed.

In the Garden of Pressing

Believers everywhere go through suffering, trials, tribulations, pressings, and persecutions. As we, Steven and Rene, have traveled the nations, we have seen much suffering. But we have also observed a component of endurance in the midst of it.

We have to go through suffering. But God did not call us to live in the valley of the shadow of death, and He walks with us through it. Too often, however, believers camp out in the valley, saying, "Woe is me!" We live under the shadow of death rather than under the shadow of His wings. We get into a pity party rather than putting our hand into Jesus' hand and allowing Him to lead us through. He wants to lead us to the other side, into vast and open places of banqueting, favor, and victory.

The question is, whom are you following? Are you following Jesus or the voice of your mindset, or the voice of your soul, or the voice of the enemy? Follow the voice of the Lord and He will get you through. Bringing you through is His heart and desire.

There will be suffering. May we say that again? There will be suffering. Yet Paul never focused on the suffering, but on the glory to be unveiled, even in the pressing. Grapes do not become juice or wine until they have been squeezed. Olives never become oil until they have been pressed.

Wherever Jesus went, He endured suffering. The Garden of Gethsemane, the grove of olive trees He visited before His arrest and crucifixion, means "oil press" or "the place of pressing," because that was where olive presses were. As Jesus allowed the Father to press and squeeze Him, He knew it was not about Himself, even though His flesh was crying out. He was saying, "It's all about You, Father."

We need to do the same thing. It is too easy to jump up and leave the olive press, but then we are only half-squeezed. God wants to complete the job and, just as when a grape is squeezed, bring about a new wine.

It is interesting that grapes are not squeezed one at a time; they are put into the press as a bunch of clusters together, to become one. Every one of those grapes looks different. Yet when we are pressed and squished together, we become something good and useful. There is a new wine that God is producing, but we have to stay in the press and allow Him to press us.

Some of the sufferings we experience are the result of mind-sets that need to be shifted.

Steven

Some years back, I was in a meeting where a gifted prophetic minister was the guest speaker, an anointed friend of the Lord. At one point, while she was preaching on discernment, she stopped to look up at heaven, and then shouted, "Will you partake of My cup of suffering?" She said this three times.

Suddenly I was hit with her words and taken into an encounter with Jesus in the heavenly realm. I saw Him walking toward me with a large chalice in His hands. I heard the prophetic leader shout again, "Will you partake of My cup of suffering?" Her voice began to change into the Lord's voice. Now all I heard was the thunderous, affectionate voice of my Jesus, saying, "Will you partake of My cup of suffering?"

I could see His face. He had a smile and those eyes full of love, and the radiance of love all around Him brought peace and joy to my heart. As He began to move closer to me, He lifted the large chalice up, asking me the same question.

Wow, Lord, I thought. *I don't think I'm able to partake of Your sufferings. Those sufferings, Lord—how could I endure?*

Jesus was persistent. He kept coming closer. I could feel the weight of His intense love. As He looked into my eyes, He asked me again with joy on his face, "Will you partake of My cup of suffering?" Lifting the chalice, He placed it to my lips.

With trembling in my whole being, I finally said, "Yes, Lord."

As I began to drink from the cup, suddenly Jesus entered into my being. He was no longer in front of me; He was now inside of me.

"Now you can endure," He said. "By My grace, you can endure My cup of sufferings and any sufferings in this life."

I realized that it is Christ in me, the hope of glory, who allows me to be able to embrace suffering.

In and of ourselves, we can never manage, but the Lord is our strength in the face of anything the enemy will throw our way. We can have confidence that Jesus is there to share with us not only His sufferings but also the incredible dimensions of His grace and glory.

Any part of our journey takes faith. How do we do that? Trust in the Lord. When we trust in the Lord, we suddenly realize what is on the inside of us.

When you say yes to Him, you have the greatest power in all the universe inside of you. The enemy works overtime to discount what is inside of you, the uncreated God of the universe. The enemy works overtime to get you to question who you really are. But in the midst of persecution and suffering, you can come to understand that Christ will bring you through. You will undergo death at some point. We all will. But it is just as King David said about going through the valley of the shadow of death. It is not death itself, but only a shadow, and Jesus is with you, who has conquered sin, hell, and the grave. His perfect blood destroyed those things and put them in a coffin forever.

This is why Peter's shadow healed people when he was not even praying for them. In truth, it was not Peter's shadow that had the power, but the One who overshadowed him. Peter knew how to rest under the shadow of the Lord's wings. That was his resting place, his refuge, where he found strength and everything he needed. It came from His relationship with Jesus and from being pressed. Once you come through the press, you get to be a witness.

We noted in chapter 4 that the disciples did not become witnesses to Jesus until Holy Spirit came upon them and filled them with power. Jesus did not say, "You will witness to people," but, "You will be my witnesses" (Acts 1:8 NIV). It is a state of being and showing the reality of Jesus. When we walk into a room, realities shift, demons manifest, and sick people get healed.

As you allow the power and presence of Holy Spirit to over-whelm you, you become a witness. Then, wherever you go, you become the radiance of Jesus. And it comes out of the garden of pressing.

The Radiance of Jesus

So what has God spoken to you? Why are you here? He is get-ting ready to perform a great move and is looking for a cluster of grapes that will submit to the pressing and the suffering. Are you willing?

Do not focus on the pressing; focus on what God wants to do once you come through. If you have said yes to Christ, then you have been called to disciple nations. And as you abide in Him, you become a carrier of the very nature of the Kingdom, which will shift nations.

> The entire universe is standing on tiptoe, yearning to see the unveiling of God's glorious sons and daughters! For against its will the universe itself has had to endure the empty futility resulting from the consequences of human sin.
>
> Romans 8:19–20 TPT

Our own sin has all creation bound up—and creation does not like to be bound up. Who likes to be in prison? Creation has a hatred for sin and disobedience; that is why it is shaking through earthquakes, fires, hurricanes, and more. We should not ignore the groaning of creation; it longs to be free.

God is not causing any of it, but He will work through it. He will take some of those things we thought were setbacks and cause them to be steppingstones into the new season. We just need to keep moving forward. "We know that all things work together for good to those who love God, to those who are the called according to His purpose" (Romans 8:28).

Just before the pressing and squishing, there is a place where we can go to meet the King in the field. It is a vast place where He is calling each one of us, a place we enter with thanksgiving and shouts of great joy, understanding that He is a good Father who has great things for us. His everlasting love will never fail. He wants to pour it out anew on His sons and daughters so we can be His witnesses.

So when you feel the intensity of warfare and testing around you, the Father of lights invites you to change your perspective. You are seated with Him in heavenly places in Christ Jesus (see Ephesians 2:6).

Steven

When I speak, I often say, "Get your head above the clouds because the Son is always shining." You can see it each time you fly in a plane, ascend above the clouds, and see that the sun is shining. When you get your head out of the clouds of noise and confusion, above the clamor of the accuser, and assume your royal position, you can see from the Father's perspective, and you are blessed with the radiance and bliss He has destined for you as his son or daughter.

God will make all things new. He is making you new. There is a dimension of transformation that the Father wants to impart to you right now:

> We all, with unveiled face, beholding as in a mirror the glory of the Lord, are being transformed into the same image from glory to glory, just as by the Spirit of the Lord.
>
> 2 Corinthians 3:18

It is not just a one-time thing. You are being made new "from glory to glory." God will shake those things that can be shaken. But as you seek His face and behold the grace and goodness of the One who sits on the throne, you will be transformed into His image by the Spirit, and your world will begin to settle. A *shalom* and grace will come upon you, even in the midst of persecution and pressing, because you are embraced by His all-encompassing, wraparound presence; you will be the radiance of Jesus to the world around you.

> "Your sun will never set again, and your moon will wane no more; the LORD will be your everlasting light, and your days of sorrow will end. Then all your people will be righteous and they will possess the land forever. They are the shoot I have planted, the work of my hands, for the display of my splendor. The least of you will become a thousand, the smallest a mighty nation. I am the LORD; in its time I will do this swiftly."
>
> Isaiah 60:20–22 NIV

This is when you become an oak of righteousness, no longer tossed to and fro by the wind, but rooted and grounded in love, to be a display for His glory and a shade and refuge for those coming in.

For those who have suffered injustice and endured difficult things, Isaiah 9:5 says, "Every warrior's boot used in battle and every garment rolled in blood will be destined for burning, will be fuel for the fire" (NIV). Every injustice, every sin, every wrong thing done to us, and every wrong thing we have done, God will use as fuel for the fire to set us ablaze with burning glory for the One who sits on the throne and who is worthy of our praise.

Journey into Perfect Love

As You reveal Your heart for me, Father, I invite the fear of the Lord over my life. It is a new day, a new season of hope, a season of victory, a season of breakthrough. Even in the middle of pain and suffering, Lord, You are speaking and leading. As I follow You, listen, and obey, You will bring me through to the other side.

Thank You, Lord, for Your transforming love and power—that perfect love that destroys fear. Send Your perfect love over me right now. Where fear has come, I break its back in Jesus' name. Let me encounter Your perfect love, heavenly Father, because You are good and Your love, mercy, and grace endure forever.

I declare that in the face of persecution, the God who created me in love and for love will join me in the fire of adversity. I will be strengthened with might in my innermost being. I declare that the fire of perfect love set ablaze inside me will overcome the flames of persecution on the outside. God is a consuming fire, and He will never leave me or forsake me.

TEN

Unified in the Flame

When the Day of Pentecost had fully come, they were all with one accord in one place. And suddenly there came a sound from heaven, as of a rushing mighty wind, and it filled the whole house where they were sitting. Then there appeared to them divided tongues, as of fire, and one sat upon each of them. And they were all filled with the Holy Spirit and began to speak with other tongues, as the Spirit gave them utterance.

Acts 2:1–4

In a world of division, hatred, and jealousy, there is only one remedy: the power of Jesus apprehending the earth with a supernatural tsunami wave of love. We are being invited into the Lord's Prayer: "Your Kingdom come; Your will be done on earth as it is in heaven."

A heavenly atmospheric shift is coming to the earth, and it will bring unity, love, and power.

"It shall come to pass afterward that I will pour out My Spirit on all flesh; your sons and your daughters shall prophesy, your old men shall dream dreams, your young men shall see visions."

Joel 2:28

This is a Joel 2:28 season, a fresh outpouring of revelation that is beginning to pour upon us, watering those weary places and creating a desire for more of Him. Jesus will cause the wind of His presence to blow, fanning into flame the embers in our hearts. The outpouring will unify and purify us, and demonstrate the power of the Kingdom—not just through signs and wonders, but through the flame of perfect love.

Hunger Attracts Heaven

That is what happened in the Upper Room after Jesus' resurrection. There were 120 sold-out lovers of God feasting on Him. They had followed Jesus for love's sake while He still walked the earth. He had seen them as they really were and who they were going to be. It was His love that compelled them.

After He was raised from the dead, Jesus told them, "I'm going to the Father, and when I do, I will send the Helper." Then He commanded them, "Go to Jerusalem and wait for the promise of the Father. Power will come upon you, and He will enable you to be witnesses and share the love of God as you have never done before."

It happened in the waiting. In the Upper Room, they pressed and pushed and prayed and cried out for ten days—and something happened. It was not their striving to make God do something, or even the words they were praying, that caused Holy

Spirit to fall. It was the hunger inside them, the fire burning inside their hearts. In that burning, yearning, and unified desire, something changed in the atmosphere over Jerusalem.

Imagine God saying, "Whoa, whoa. Something's happening. Such affection is rising up! Do You smell that, Holy Spirit? Jesus, come here, smell this."

With the unity in the room and hunger inside the disciples—wanting the more, wanting the fullness, wanting the promise—the whole atmosphere began to change until, on the Day of Pentecost, God said, "All right, Holy Spirit." Then, *Whoosh!* Into the Upper Room came the sound of a mighty, rushing wind, and flames of fire landed on each of the 120 believers (see Acts 2:3).

We believe the tongues of fire appeared on their heads as a sign that Holy Spirit was changing the way they thought. That is what fire does—it burns and destroys those things that hinder love from being seen and experienced in its fullness. It brings transformation. And it sets us free.

As that wind blew in on the Day of Pentecost, it blew old mindsets out the window, and it blew on the embers and flame flickering inside each heart. They were longing for love, for friendship, for an ongoing relationship with the One they loved. They were longing to stand face to face with Him as they had before. And when the wind and flames came into the room, the little flames within them became a consuming fire.

God wants to do the same with you today. He wants to blow away old thinking and old mindsets and awaken the truth of who He is and who you are. Isaiah 43:18–19 says, "Do not remember the former things, nor consider the things of old. Behold, I will do a new thing, now it shall spring forth." So forget your past. Forget what people said about you. Forget the hard times. Even now the freshness of new life is springing forth—the green reality of who He is and who you are.

When we realize our desperate need for God, it produces a divine hunger. This hunger no longer comes from a place of lack but from the table of God's abundant love, in which we "taste and see" how good God is and that we must have more.

Jesus promised, "I have come to give you everything in abundance, more than you expect—life in its fullness until you overflow!" (John 10:10 TPT). The Greek word for *life* is a form of the word *zóé*, expressing the highest and best that Jesus gives to His beloved saints. Jesus wants *zóé* life to erupt in and through us, so we can live the abundant life He died for. It comes from the place of understanding and being established in His love. Then, when we are set ablaze with His all-consuming fire, we will never be the same.

Pentecost came during the Feast of Weeks, the celebration of the wheat harvest when Israelites came from all over to bring their firstfruits offerings to the Lord in Jerusalem. As believers in Jesus, we know there is coming a harvest of souls. A fresh Pentecost in our day will release hearts to burn and then bring in the harvest—a gathering of people who will grasp how amazing God's love is, and who will come into the revelation of Jesus Christ as Lord and King.

The Miracle of Unity

Jewish tradition says that the first Pentecost coincided with the day God gave Moses the Ten Commandments on Mount Sinai. Moses climbed up the mountain and for forty days spent time with God. In that place, there was an intimacy and unraveling, where God spoke to him, revealed what He expected of the Israelites, and gave him the Ten Commandments.

The Hebrews were afraid because they saw and heard fire, thunder, and lightning on Mount Sinai, and Moses was right in the middle of it. He was receiving a revelation of the holiness and love of God, who was revealing Himself to the Israelites and making covenant with them as His special people. God said, "If you obey me fully and keep my covenant, then out of all nations you will be my treasured possession" (Exodus 19:5 NIV). And when Moses came down from the mountain with those tablets of stone, on which God had inscribed the Ten Commandments, he carried the revelation of the written Word of God.

Moses alone, up on the mountain, experienced the all-consuming fire of God. But fifteen hundred years later, when Holy Spirit was poured out on the believers gathered in the Upper Room, not just one but every one of them experienced the fire. And from the outpouring on the 120 who had gathered there, we celebrate the birth of the Church.

What is the Church? Not just a building we go to. Not even a gathering of believers. On the contrary, when Jesus referred to the Church, He used a word that can be found throughout the New Testament—the word *ekklesia*, a Greek term for "called-out ones." *Ekklesia* was an assembly of people who governed and made legislation, decrees, and declarations. So in Matthew 16:18, when Jesus said, "I will build My church," He was saying: "I'm going to build My *ekklesia*, and the gates of hell will not prevail against it. These are the called-out ones awakened to the truth of My Word, who will proclaim the truth throughout the earth."

In the Upper Room, then, as that group of believers fasted, shouted, decreed, declared, and worshiped, hunger and longing were being awakened inside them because they knew that soon God was going to bring the promise. A realm of heaven would be opened up, as in Isaiah 64:1: "Oh, that you would rend the heavens and come down" (NIV).

So in the Upper Room, as they waited, there was excitement, zeal, and probably even, at times, just silence. But there was not only hunger in that place; there was oneness and unity. Acts 2:1 says, "They were all with one accord in one place." This was, in and of itself, part of the miracle, because if we really look at the disciples, we see how different they were from each other.

We have Matthew, a tax collector. We have Peter, Andrew, James, and John, all fishermen. We have the women, including Mary, Jesus' mother, and Mary Magdalene. And we have James and Judas (Jude), who wrote the book of Jude—Jesus' brothers, sons of Mary, who did not even believe at first that Jesus was the Messiah. It made no sense to them because they had grown up with Him. Yet they were two of the 120 waiting in the Upper Room.

Even with how eclectic this crowd was, the oneness that came as they worshiped God in Spirit and truth, as they chose mindfully to set their gaze on the things of heaven, caused them to put aside their differences. They were about the one thing— David's cry in Psalm 27:4 (NIV):

> One thing I ask from the LORD, this only do I seek: that I may dwell in the house of the LORD all the days of my life, to gaze on the beauty of the LORD and to seek him in his temple.

That is what was happening in the Upper Room. The disciples' seeking and fascination with the grace and goodness of God created oneness.

An interesting compound word in the Greek, *homothuma-don*, is translated "in one accord," and it means "rushing along in unison." *Homothumadon* is used ten times in the book of Acts. It is like an orchestra with many different instruments and many different sounds, but all of it together creating a oneness.

In the sound of the 120 shouting and worshiping in the Upper Room, there was oneness and unity; it was *homothumadon*. The disciples were rushing alongside one another in unison. Where did the rushing begin? It began in their hearts as lovers of Jesus. As their sounds rushed along together in unison, heaven was compelled to join in.

And suddenly that sound came from heaven, that mighty, rushing wind, as divided tongues of fire rested on each one of the disciples. The heavens were torn open and Holy Spirit came down.

The Church as we know it did not yet exist. There were still old mindsets and old ways of doing things. But as the Spirit blew in, He blew old mindsets out and brought in a fresh wave of God's presence. The Spirit of wisdom and revelation and burning was unlocked and released.

The Reality of Heaven

When John baptized Jesus in the Jordan River, the heavens opened up and the Spirit of God came down in the form of the dove of *shalom*, resting on the King of kings, the Prince of Peace. Several years later, Holy Spirit did not come on the disciples in the form of a gentle dove; He came in the form of wind and fire.

As He descended on those in the Upper Room, they rejoiced and began speaking in other languages. The Bible says that people from many different nations heard their own languages and asked mockingly, "Are not all these who speak Galileans?" (Acts 2:7). It was as if they were saying, "What are these bumpkins doing, speaking our language?" Others mocked them: "They are full of new wine" (verse 13). But still others said, "Whoa, that's good news right there. How do you guys know that? And how do you know my language?"

The believers continued to worship God, speaking in many languages about the wonders of God and His Kingdom. The reality of heaven was poured down onto those believers, spilling out of the Upper Room onto the streets of Jerusalem, just as Jesus had prophesied. They were baptized with fire and with power.

Then Peter addressed the crowd—those who mocked and those who were in sincere awe and wonder. He explained that these disciples were not drunk with wine but filled with Holy Spirit and with fire.

"What you're seeing isn't an issue of alcohol," he said, "but Holy Spirit coming down as He promised. You're seeing and experiencing the love of God that goes beyond your comprehension. I want to invite you into this reality. This is what was prophesied by the prophet Joel." And he took them right back to the power of the Word of God:

"In the last days it shall be, God declares, that I will pour out my Spirit on all flesh, and your sons and your daughters shall prophesy, and your young men shall see visions, and your old men shall dream dreams; even on my male servants and female servants in those days I will pour out my Spirit, and they shall prophesy."

Acts 2:17–18 esv

The believers stepped into another dimension that day, a dimension of heaven.

Yet another dimension is coming when God will rend the heavens even more widely—because He wants Holy Spirit to fall not just on the ones who were in that Upper Room in Jerusalem but on every person. God's promise in Joel "that I will pour out my Spirit on all flesh" is available to every single person who says yes to the King of kings.

Fire and Wind

God wants to release a fresh baptism of fire upon His united Church again. May we celebrate and rejoice at being filled and overflowing with all that He has in store! God has much more for each one of us as we become one with Him and with one another.

And God wants the wind of His Spirit to blow on the embers of our hearts and to rekindle us with the love and passion that come from heavenly places. It is nothing we can conjure up. If that were the case, God would never have had to send the promised Spirit.

Fire gets hot; it burns. We were created to be set on fire by His love, so that people around us who do not yet know Jesus are drawn to the fire inside us. This fire brings comfort, warmth, strength, and peace.

And as the wind blew into the Upper Room, it stirred things up. It was like a farmer in those days who would use the wind at threshing time. After beating the wheat seed to loosen the husk, or chaff, he would throw a basket of beaten grain and chaff into the air, and the wind would blow the chaff, which was lighter, away.

That is what God is doing with the Church. He wants to blow the chaff away. A rushing is coming—*homothumadon*—and He is looking for ones who will rush along in unison. Unity, not uniformity, is what He is looking for. Because—like the disciples and like Paul's description in 1 Corinthians 12 of the different parts of the body—we are all different. We are fingers, toes, eyes, and noses. Each part looks different and would look weird by itself. But putting them all together creates an amazing display of God's goodness and grace.

As unity is unlocked, we will begin to function like the Body of Christ, no longer dismembered or hobbling along on one leg (or no legs!). He is bringing us together in completeness so we can move together as one—so in that place of rushing along in unison, the world will say, "Look at that! That's the kind of love I want."

In this day and hour, God is erasing those lines that religion puts in place. Those religious structures say, "No, you've got to go to four years of seminary, and after that, get your doctorate. And then you can finally preach the Gospel." That is funny, because those ones in the Upper Room had just been filled with Holy Spirit, and they did not sign up for rabbinical school; they just started preaching, and with wisdom, revelation, and conviction.

Today God is pouring out Holy Spirit on sons and daughters—all those who have said yes to Jesus. That neighbor you dislike will get whacked by the power and glory of God's goodness. That co-worker who annoys you—guess what? This is her inheritance. Even we old ones, we are going to have dreams. Young people, get ready for visions. They are yours. Age does not make a difference in what God is doing.

The only requirement is saying yes to Jesus and believing the truth of who He is. As we believe in Him, we see the fullness of

His Spirit. And when He comes in power, we are given the ability, like the disciples on the Day of Pentecost, to be witnesses. Not to *go* and witness, but to *be* witnesses.

It makes no difference if you are male or female, young or old, the poorest of the poor or a multi-billionaire. God is no respecter of persons. Recall what Jesus said about Holy Spirit:

> "Which of you fathers, if your son asks for a fish, will give him a snake instead? Or if he asks for an egg, will give him a scorpion? If you then, though you are evil, know how to give good gifts to your children, how much more will your Father in heaven give the Holy Spirit to those who ask him?"
>
> Luke 11:11–13 NIV

It starts with asking. In the Upper Room, they were asking and they were hungry and they were in unity, because they knew the promise of Jesus: "It is better that I go away, because the Father will send the promised Holy Spirit. And He is going to set you in a whole new place, and blow your mind and heart and will and emotions."

Through Holy Spirit, God brings us into alignment with who He created us to be. As we are filled with His presence and power as His sons and daughters, we become bearers of the Good News and the hope ambassadors the world longs to see and hear. We come with the good word, the encouragement, the strength, and the grace that allow them—and us!—to be more than conquerors.

Filled to Overflowing

On the Day of Pentecost, Peter explained the Good News of Jesus, the Messiah, whom they had crucified but whom had

God raised to life. Straight from the Scripture, Peter unpacked the reality of the Gospel of the Kingdom. Since it was during Passover that Jesus had been crucified, many of those listening to Peter had been in Jerusalem and seen firsthand what had happened.

As Peter spoke, the people were pierced in their hearts by the Word of God. Their response: "Oh, oh, oh, that pains me. It was me! It was my sin that hung Jesus on that cross. What must I do to be saved?" They began to ask this question before Peter even got to that point. He responded,

"Repent and be baptized, every one of you, in the name of Jesus Christ for the forgiveness of your sins. And you will receive the gift of the Holy Spirit."

Acts 2:38 NIV

The word *repent* here is translated from the Greek word *metanoia*, from which we get the word *metamorphosis*. It speaks of changing direction from the pathway of destruction that we had been on before we came to know Christ; it also speaks of changing a mindset, so we begin to see God as He really is.

The people of Jerusalem that day were filled to overflowing, as Jesus had promised: "He who believes in Me, as the Scripture has said, out of his heart will flow rivers of living water" (John 7:38). That is the kind of filling He wants to give us, too, so we become a blessing that overflows. Just as David wrote, "My cup runs over" (Psalm 23:5), God wants us to be running over with the fullness of Him and all His promises, which are *yes* and *amen* (see 2 Corinthians 1:20).

So prepare Him room. He wants *you* to be that overflowing cup, so that when you go out into the community, you are bubbling over with joy. God wants to pour out His Spirit afresh on you today. How much more will your Father in heaven give Holy Spirit to those who ask Him? Is there an asking today? Is there a want-to today?

After Peter and John had been imprisoned and threatened for their faith, the disciples cried out "with one accord" (Acts 4:24) for God to fill them with boldness. At this point, they had been preaching the Gospel, had witnessed amazing miracles, and had seen many people believing in Jesus—yet they knew there was more. The result? "They were all filled with the Holy Spirit, and they spoke the word of God with boldness" (verse 31).

God also wants to pour out "the more" on us, because when "the more" comes, we set aside our own selfish desires, grab hold of the Father's desires (since He is the One who put those desires inside us in the first place), and people get saved.

When Moses came down the mountain with the tablets of stone with the Law of the Lord, he found the Israelites giving themselves over to idol worship. They had witnessed how God had delivered them miraculously out of Egypt and parted the Red Sea, yet their hearts were already turning back to old ways. Moses, distraught, threw down the stone tablets. His heart was broken because they chose to worship the golden calf, breaking God's very first commandment. Three thousand people died that day (see Exodus 32:28).

Fast forward to the Day of Pentecost and the birth of the Church. This time God did not come down to write on stone tablets, but on the tablets of human hearts. Three thousand people were saved that day (see Acts 2:41).

When God comes down, He changes the atmosphere. When God comes down, there is a revelation of His love that does not ever fail or fade. He wants to do it today. He wants to pour out

His Spirit and fill you anew because there is a lost and dying world out there. They do not need to hear doom and gloom. The Bible is full of Good News, and He wants you full of Good News, too.

Being filled with God's Spirit brings life, hope, and strength. It heals communities and brings grace, power, and the reality of what Jesus died for—to deliver us from sin and death and restore us to a relationship with Father God.

So if you want Holy Spirit today, just ask. He is available right now. You may even begin to feel His presence, a peace that goes beyond your comprehension.

When Paul says to be "filled with Holy Spirit" (Ephesians 5:18), the Greek word is *plērousthe*, being filled, denoting the ongoing, perpetual infilling of Holy Spirit. The disciples, as we have seen, did not have a one-time filling and encounter with Holy Spirit; they were filled many times.

God's desire is to fill you, too, continually, so you become one with Him, wrapped in His perfect love.

Journey into Perfect Love

This interactive spiritual exercise will help you move from hunger to abundance to overflow.

Stirring Up Personal Hunger

- Start by acknowledging your need for more of God.
- Ask God to stir up His divine hunger within you.
- Agree with the revelation that in God's presence there is no lack and that He alone satisfies.

Feasting on the Abundance

- Imagine the banqueting table of the God of love, full of everything you need in Him.
- Acknowledge the abundance He provides for you. Whatever your soul hungers for can be satisfied in Him.
- "Taste and see" spiritually that the Lord is good in every area of your life. This is a place of communing and receiving from the abundance of His love.

Filled to Overflowing

- As you are filled up to overflowing, ask Holy Spirit to provide opportunities for what you have received to overflow onto others throughout your day.
- Thank God for the oneness and unity His love brings to your heart and to the world around you.
- Ask God to help you find a tribe of Christian "foodies" who also desire to feast on the Lord together.

Holy Spirit, fall on me afresh right now as I am being unified in the fire of perfect love. I declare that I am becoming one with the Lord, and He is making me one with the Body of Christ. As Holy Spirit falls afresh on me with dunamis *power and glory, I am being satisfied and filled to overflowing, never to be the same, unified in His perfect peace, grace, power, and love.*

This interactive exercise is also available at www.globalpresence .com/PerfectLove.

ELEVEN

Firebrands Compelled to Go

"I have come to set the earth on fire, and how I wish it were already ablaze with fiery passion for God!"

Luke 12:49 TPT

The amazing journey of becoming one with the fire of perfect love does something on the inside of us. It awakens us, recalibrates us, aligns us, and fills us with our Father's perfect love, which overflows from our hearts to the world around us. Reaching out to those who do not yet know Him is no longer a program or religious obligation, but an incredible overflow of love.

As we set our hearts continually to gaze on the beauty of who Jesus is, we are transformed by love that compels us to go. We, Steven and Rene, coined the phrase "gaze and go." Every time we seek Him, we get a bit more of His heart. Fascinated by His face, gazing on His glorious splendor and all that He is, we cannot help but be moved by the things that move Him.

Our hearts start to burn with His passion to see others come into this amazing reality. It is the gazing that compels us to go and be witnesses of His great love.

Grabbing hold of the greatest commandment—loving God with all that we are—will always lead to the fulfillment of the Great Commission: going into all the world. If we try to obey the second commandment, on the other hand—loving our neighbors as ourselves—disconnected from the intimacy that comes from gazing on the Lord, we will tend to get burned out.

We are going to see a change in this era with a generation of "laid-down lovers" who, in the midst of going, do not lose their gaze. This is how Jesus operated during His ministry on earth. He did only what He saw the Father doing, He said only what He heard the Father saying, and He prayed only what He heard the Father praying (see John 5:19). Jesus' heart was always connected with the Father's, and from that place He was moved not by compulsion or religious duty, but by compassion.

Compelled by Compassion

We are invited into the same dimension in which Jesus walked. Matthew 14:14 shows that Jesus, even in the thick of the crowds, did not become overwhelmed but was moved by the Father's heart. He was moved *through* the Father's heart. And He was moved to *be* the Father's heart. Moved by compassion, He healed all who were sick—those who had diseases and those who had issues of the heart.

We are being challenged and commissioned in the very same way—to be moved by compassion, motivated from a place of loving God with all that we are, to go love and heal the world around us.

Before He left the earth, Jesus promised His disciples that He would not leave them orphaned but would send the Comforter. That happened when Holy Spirit was poured out on the Day of Pentecost. Since then, He has not stopped filling those who are His friends and lovers.

Jesus said about the person who believes in Him, "Greater works than these he will do, because I go to My Father" (John 14:12). Think of the things Jesus did in the Gospels. How amazing is it that we will not only do more things than those, but even greater things? It is when we are moved and compelled by love that we will see these greater things released.

Jesus endured the cross "for the joy that was set before Him" (Hebrews 12:2). *We* were the joy set before Him! He saw your face and mine as He hung on the cross. It was love that compelled Him to offer up His life so that we can live.

So now, as we make Jesus the joy set before us, and as we gaze at our resurrected King, we enter into His heart's longing for the harvest. We see through the fiery eyes of Christ that every human being on the planet was created in God's image with the opportunity to become a son and daughter—a history-making, world-changing individual for the glory of God and His Kingdom.

Compelled by the Reality of Heaven and Hell

Steven

Many years back, I had an encounter that changed my understanding of the reality of the joy that was set before Jesus.

One evening just before going to sleep, Rene and I were praying and thanking God for all the things we were seeing and that we were able to be part of for the sake of His Kingdom. I began to feel my spirit being removed from my body, similar to what Paul described in 2 Corinthians 12.

"Rene!" I exclaimed. "Something is happening here!"

As I stared at the ceiling, it began to get farther and farther away, and I knew I was being taken into an encounter with God.

The next thing I knew, I was no longer in my bedroom, but standing in a corridor, a kind of tunnel of white stone, somewhat roughly hewn, like the catacombs in Rome. At the very end of the tunnel was an incredible, beaming light of love radiating out toward me.

Suddenly, from behind, a massive angel, maybe fifteen or sixteen feet tall, grabbed my hand and began to walk me down the corridor. With each step, I sensed a greater dimension of being overcome by God's love. The rough-hewn catacomb floor began to become shiny and white, like a finished corridor of marble.

As we got closer to the light, I began to feel vibrations of love and hope and excitement and joy. When we reached the end of the corridor, where the shaft of love was beaming down, the angel pointed into the light, and I looked up into it. It was almost painfully bright, but all I felt was amazing, loving light filling my being.

Suddenly a dove descended out of the light and landed on my shoulder. I was overcome by the weight of goodness, glory, compassion, and kindness.

The dove said to me, "Turn around."

As I turned, I saw a chasm behind me that had not been there a moment before. I almost fell into it. As I caught my balance, I began to sense an evil presence and smell a vile, sulfur-like smell. As I looked down into the chasm, I saw a wicked-looking creature about forty feet below me, laughing and laughing and laughing—a maniacal laugh full of hatred and mockery.

I asked the dove, "What is he laughing at?"

Then, in a moment, something dropped rapidly past me from above. Then something else rushed past me. And I heard, "Help me! Help me! Help me!"

As I began to grasp what was going on, I could see that they were actually human beings dropping past me, one by one, screaming, "Help me! Help me! Help me!" But I was unable to help them. That painful reality gripped my heart as it became clear that they had already made their choice.

The screaming and terror I felt from each person zooming by me was horrific. I knew what I was seeing was not hypothetical. I was being allowed to see real people. One by one, to this day, I can still remember each of their faces. They were descending into the abyss of the fiery place that was designed and created for Satan himself.

The reality is, God did not send any of those individuals to the place of separation, to hell, where there is burning and fire and gnashing of teeth. I knew it was the free-will choice of each of them, and that they had chosen not to believe that Jesus Christ is the way, the truth, and the life, and the only way to Almighty God, the Father.

As another one fell by, I remember the pain inside my heart. I was beginning to feel in a small way how the Father must feel with the pain of eternal separation—that those He created in His image would not live with Him in eternity, but in this place of burning and torment forever. I was gripped by the pain and sadness of the Father's heart.

This encounter, as it faded away, haunted me for weeks on end, as I saw the faces and heard the screams, and all the while the enemy mocking and laughing.

The reality is, Satan's day is coming when there will be no more laughter from him, just eternal torment, for he will find his final place in the lake of fire.

And it is important to understand that God does not send any human being to hell. In His goodness and love, He has given every person free will to accept or reject His gift of salvation. Those who receive Jesus as Savior are restored to a relationship with God and will spend eternity with Him, where every tear will be wiped away and there will be no more death, sorrow, or pain.

Heaven and hell are real places, and our personal choice determines where we will spend eternity. But God is a good Father, filled with love and longing for His creatures, made in His image, to accept His love and place their faith in His Son.

Gripped by the encounter I had experienced, and sensing the love and ache in the Father's heart, I have been compelled as never before to share His love with the world around me.

May the reality of heaven and hell, and the yearning of God the Father, who is "not willing that any should perish" (2 Peter 3:9), compel you also.

Firebrands Arising

There is a divine mystery—a secret surprise that has been concealed from the world for generations, but now it's being revealed, unfolded and manifested for every holy believer to experience. Living within you is the Christ who floods you with the expectation of glory! This mystery of Christ, embedded

within us, becomes a heavenly treasure chest of hope filled with
the riches of glory for his people, and God wants everyone to
know it!

Colossians 1:26–27 TPT

As these verses make clear, the riches of Christ's glory are
being revealed in our lives—a treasure chest of hope to the
world around us. We are set apart for such a time as this. God
is marking a generation of burning ones who have been consumed by the flame of first love. We are being branded by His
love to become firebrands who will spread the fiery passion of
Christ across the earth.

What is a firebrand? Someone passionate about a particular cause, typically inciting change and taking radical action.
Today God is raising up firebrands who have been touched by
love and branded by His goodness. We are the generation who
will take radical action to see His Kingdom come with love,
grace, and power.

The prophet Isaiah had an incredible heavenly encounter in
which he saw the Lord "high and lifted up" (Isaiah 6:1) and
became overwhelmed by how pure and holy God is. During
this encounter in the heavenly realm of God in all His majesty, Isaiah saw and heard the seraphim, those burning ones,
crying, "Holy, holy, holy is the LORD of hosts" (verse 3). He
realized that his lips and the very depths of his being were
unclean.

This is what happens when we enter God's presence. It brings
everything into the light.

Then one of the seraphim came with a coal from the altar
of God, and with it touched Isaiah's lips. In a moment, Isaiah's mouth—his very words—were purified and cleansed by

this burning flame of love. The prophet had the opportunity to actually taste and see how good God's fiery love is. This encounter marked him in that moment, purifying him to be a firebrand with a voice of righteousness and purity to his generation.

It is profound that as Isaiah looked up, seeing what was going on in the heavenly realm, he heard the conversation of the Father, Son, and Holy Spirit—the Triune, magnificent, uncreated God. Caught in the swirls of His love and glory, Isaiah heard this conversation: "Whom shall I send, and who will go for Us?" (Isaiah 6:8).

God asked this question not because He did not know the answer, but because He wanted Isaiah to hear the desire of His heart: *Will you go? Let's do this together.* Out of Isaiah's encounter with this amazing, beautiful Love, he responded, "Here am I! Send me."

God is doing the same with us. He wants to cleanse and purify us to become more like Him, transformed from glory to glory. Those He marks and purifies will go forth and compel others to say yes and amen to His goodness.

This firebrand generation—not a particular age group, but people alive today—will be marked by God's purity, love, and holy power. As we hear the conversation of heaven—the invitation of God saying, "Who are the ones who will go for us?"—this firebrand generation will have the same response Isaiah did: "Here I am, God. Send me." We will be moved not by compulsion or religious duty; this army of "laid-down lovers" will be moved by the beauty of God's amazing love and compassion. We will reflect the heart of God and live from the revelation that even our weak love moves His heart. And we will become the movement of God on the earth.

Sharing God's Love As a Lifestyle

Rene

Evangelism is a lifestyle, not a program. It is about people touched by the love of God. Please don't misunderstand—there are intentional times of equipping the saints in evangelism, and it is important to learn to step out in those ways. But rather than being confined to a program, sharing God's love can become a natural part of our lifestyle.

Steven and I consider it a privilege and joy to release God's anointing over masses of people, bringing salvation and freedom to many. But if it is only about ministry from a platform, we are missing the point. It is when we are compelled by love that God's power is released through our everyday lives, especially to the people closest to us.

Before receiving Christ, Steven had gone through a hard divorce with much pain and fighting. He and his ex-wife both loved their son, Justin (who captured my heart as well). But Justin was caught in the middle of his parents' contention. We knew that things needed to change for his sake. And as newly saved Christians, we had confidence that if God could save us, He could save Steven's ex-wife as well. We began to pray fervently for her salvation.

There is much to this story, but the most important thing is how God came into our blended family and did something beyond what we could ask or imagine. Not only was Steven's ex-wife saved, but we were the ones who got to lead her to the Lord, and I became a mentor to her. We came to love each other and became good friends with a lot of mutual respect.

Compelled by love, Steven and I found God's power released to save someone close to us and heal our blended family.

Everyone can have a heart for the lost. And there is not only one way to reach out. You just need to find how God will do it through you in a way that is natural—through your gifts, talents, creativity, and the sphere of influence He has put you in.

I did not think I was good at evangelism because I am not good at "cold calling." I tend to be better with relational or prophetic evangelism. I get a heart tug for someone and a compelling desire to share something with him or her. Then my prophetic anointing kicks in, and I sense part of God's heart to share with that person. This is different from just walking up to somebody.

I have found, however, that it is not just one way or the other. Each of us can evangelize in a way that comes naturally. As Global Presence teams go to the streets, I love being paired with someone with a bold personality who can just go up to anybody. At some point, as my partner is interacting with someone, I start to sense what God has for this person—because God really does have a word for everybody.

We may think of "mission" as going to other countries. In reality, the mission field is in our own backyards. It is every time we leave our houses. God has divine appointments for us every day. The more in tune we are to His heart, the more in tune we will be with how He wants to touch people through us with His love.

It is a regular occurrence for me to look out the window and see Steven praying over people who service our property. One time when the guys came to pump out our septic tank, I looked out the window and saw the man Steven was praying for almost fall over under the power of God. *Oh no*, I thought, *he's going to fall into the septic stuff!* (That got me praying, too!) The man was set free from addiction that day.

Another time we hired a guy to help us with some landscaping. At the end of the day, Steven offered to pray for his business and asked him about his health.

The landscaper replied, "My health is fine, but my father's is not."

Steven replied, "Tell me about that."

"My father lives in El Salvador. He's been diagnosed with stage four cancer, and the doctors say there's nothing they can do."

Steven began to share with the man and his son, who had come with him, about other cases of cancer that we have seen eradicated by the power and love of Christ. Steven said that the power of Christ's love would do the same for this man's father, and added, "Let's agree together in prayer." Then he began to make declarations of faith, proclaiming life, freedom, and healing over the landscaper's father.

The man told Steven he was beginning to feel vibrations of God's love. He and his son teared up as the power and presence of God came on them. Then Steven said he sensed a release of the father from the bondage of the demonic spirit behind the cancer.

"It's finished!" Steven exclaimed. "He's healed, in Jesus' name!"

And he was. A few months later, when the landscaper came back to give a quote on some additional work, he told Steven with the biggest smile and tears of joy, "I have to tell you. Remember when we prayed for my father, and the doctors said they couldn't do anything? Today Dad is completely cancer-free. I know it was from those powerful prayers, and I give all the glory to Jesus for healing my father."

So the mission field is all around us. We get to be extensions of God's love released in our neighborhoods, schools, and communities.

In the introduction to this book, Steven and I wrote that we got to partner with God's heart at the University of Wisconsin in Madison by establishing a house of prayer called The Furnace. It was a dedicated place of God's presence, an outpost of His love on the biggest party street on the campus. It was a furnace of fiery affection where the incense of worship rose day and night, releasing the beauty of who God is.

As we chose to be burning ones—firebrands!—we burned for others to know God's love. Several days a week, we came to The Furnace to be saturated in God's presence in worship and prayer, and then went right back out the door to release the love that had filled us up. Week in and week out, we saw many people encounter the love of Christ. Drunk college students sobered up as God touched their hearts. Tears streamed down their faces as we prophesied that God saw them, knew them, and created them for love, friendship, and greatness. In the midst of wild partying in the streets, we saw instantaneous healings.

We made love the goal. Jesus did the saving; we were simply mouthpieces of the reality of the kindness and goodness of God, a really good Father. We saw miracles, signs, and wonders week in and week out as people encountered the love of God.

Steven

Sharing God's love is a family affair. It became normal for our daughter, Elizabeth, to go out with us at a young age to look for God's treasures in the streets of our city. She began prophesying at age three, and releasing prophetic words in the streets with us by age nine. The messages she released had such purity and power that a large college football player was taken aback, tears running down his face, as she spoke words from our heavenly Father's heart over him.

Another time Elizabeth and I saw a man in a wheelchair shaking a can for money. As we approached him, Elizabeth said, "Dad, Jesus said we're supposed to pray for him."

We stopped and asked him how he was doing and what was going on. Then Elizabeth asked him if we could pray for him for healing.

How can you deny a child who is asking to pray for you? So he began to share his story—how he had been in a motorcycle accident and had broken his back in four places. He had been in a wheelchair ever since.

Once again we asked if we could pray with him for his healing, and he agreed.

As we extended the love and kindness of God, we began to release healing into his back and into those vertebrae, into the pain and inflammation. We spoke the name of Jesus over and over. I could tell he was experiencing the love of Jesus poured upon him. Then we asked him to do something he had not been able to do, and welcomed him to stand up out of his wheelchair.

As he stood to his feet, his smile was coupled with a look of wonder on his face, like *What just happened?!* Then he started to move around and shift his back.

"Do something you couldn't do," I repeated.

"I am."

"What do you mean?"

He looked at us with tears in his eyes. "I haven't been able to stand this long in four years! I couldn't stand even for a moment without severe pain. But the pain that was in my back even a moment ago is completely gone!"

The simple faith of a child extended the love of God to a man that day. There was beauty and simplicity in Elizabeth's faith. She was so filled with love that she became love and released love.

Using Our Unique Talents and Abilities

Sometimes we miss what is obvious in our lives just because it comes naturally. But we can ask the Lord how we can use our natural talents and abilities to share His love with others.

A great example of this is an amazing couple who got radically saved in one of our meetings at Global Presence. They had referred to themselves previously as "spiritual freelancers," meaning they were open to anything and everything—good, bad, and deceptive. But all it took was an encounter with the loving presence of the one true and living God for them to become sold-out lovers of Jesus.

This couple were successful attorneys and owned a law firm. Now, as new believers, the more they pressed into God, the more their hearts were awakened to His unfailing love, and they encountered His goodness and kindness. They began to share Christ with some of their clients. In fact, they were so compelled to share His love that they asked if they could offer a free legal clinic within our Apostolic Center (which is dedicated to personal and societal transformation, centered in God's presence and biblical values, with demonstrations of His love, grace, and supernatural power). To do this, they had to change their law firm hours from five days a week to four, so they could have a day to offer free legal advice.

Even so, the firm continued to flourish supernaturally, while they enjoyed an incredible opportunity to bring the love of Christ to the community. Many who might never have come into a church came in looking for help and found the legal advice they needed. And as their fear went away, an opening was created for our friends to share the love of Christ and lead them to Jesus, right there in the legal clinic.

The legal clinic drew attention in our region, in the press, and even from a member of the high court in the state.

Another couple with whom we are close friends are making an impact on their city in two ways: spiritually, with a beautiful prayer room community; and in the marketplace, with a successful chain of restaurants. The prayer room serves as a beautiful place of worship, a fragrant offering to God, where believers intercede on behalf of their city and nation and actually influence legislation through prayer and decrees. They have seen great shifts for God's Kingdom in answer to their prayers.

And our friends have been able to share the Gospel in their restaurants, where employees and customers alike encounter the goodness of God. Before a store opens for the day, employees are invited to gather in a circle for a time of prayer. On one particularly chaotic day, an employee who was not even a Christian said, "Can we circle up and do that thing?"

These are just a few examples of how four friends are using their natural talents and abilities in their sphere of influence in order to make an impact.

Go Into All Your World

Jesus commissioned us to "go and make disciples of all nations" (Matthew 28:19 NIV). But we often confuse that as meaning, "Quit your job, become a missionary, and go live in the bush somewhere." What Jesus was saying was, "As you go into all your world, make disciples." You may be called to go to a distant place at the end of the earth. But your world starts right outside your door. You can make disciples at home or across the street, of your neighbor or your co-worker.

We, Steven and Rene, have seen God move in amazing ways over the years. From a hut in Africa to a board room in Asia to our very own living room, God has shown up with His saving grace and unfailing love. And God is marking us to be carriers of His Good News. He is branding us with His amazing love that we not only tell His story, but we *become* His story. He says, "Be strong and courageous."

So don't let fear steal your joy and prevent you from being the light of Christ in the midst of darkness. Showing the world God's beautiful love and helping people encounter His presence is far better than anything else on earth.

Jesus is the remedy. And He is setting apart the people who will believe Him, and believe with Him, that His love never fails.

Touching the Hearts of Kings

Steven

God began to whisper to us many years ago, especially since we had been overcome by the reality of poverty in many of the nations to which we had traveled. The Lord said, "You have done well to go after the poor of the earth, but I am calling you to the poor in spirit of the earth. Even as you have loved the 'down-and-outers,' I am calling you to the 'up-and-outers,' those who sit in high places of influence and authority and nations."

We realized that one of the things the Lord was saying was that if we can touch the heart of a king, we can change a nation. A king might be the mayor of your city, a leader in Hollywood in arts and entertainment, the head of the school board, the CEO of a company, the president or leader of a nation, or anyone who makes decisions.

We saw this firsthand in Ghana, West Africa, where we had the opportunity to touch the heart of a king. It all started with a dangerous prayer: "Lord, what are You doing and how can we become part of it?" (When we ask this question, Jesus shows up and does all kinds of amazing things above anything we can think or imagine.)

In fact, our first trip to Ghana happened through a young man studying at the university near us. He dreamed of being part of a community that would go back with him to love the Ghanaian people and bring transformation, and he found the answer to his prayer in our ministry and our church community.

Rene and I prayed and listened to the Lord as we made our way into remote areas of Ghana. I began to ask Him if He wanted us to do anything in this nation on an ongoing basis. Observing the people and the poverty, I had the sense that the Lord was about to show up and show off.

After five hours of travel in an old Toyota coaster bus on bumpy roads riddled with potholes, we reached the village where our young friend had grown up. Protocol in Ghanaian tribal society dictates that, before any humanitarian help can be given within a community, permission must be sought from the chiefs and elders. So we stopped to meet with the local "paramount chief" (a local chieftain or monarch) and elders.

We sat before them at the paramount chief's palace and told them the reason we were there—to share the love and healing power of Jesus Christ with the village, which our native team member so loved, and to help equip pastors and leaders in the region. The chief and elders granted us permission to be in their village.

Before the meeting was over, we asked the leaders how we could pray for them. We told them that Jesus is the Healer and mentioned some of the amazing miracles we had seen.

The paramount chief was the first to raise his hand. We prayed for him, and he was miraculously healed by the power of God. We proceeded to pray for all who needed a touch from the Lord. And then we released a blessing over the leadership and entire community.

The leaders looked stunned. I knew they sensed the presence of Almighty God.

The paramount chief called us back to his palace the following day for another meeting. We prophesied over him, spoke God's heart to him, and shared the vision—which I had drawn out on a page in my journal—of a ministry base that would better the community. We knew he wanted the presence of the Lord, which he had encountered the previous day, to be cultivated in his village.

As Rene and the team and I continued to demonstrate the reality of God's love, after two years of coming and building and partnering, I had the pleasure of leading the king to Jesus and seeing him baptized in the fire of Holy Spirit.

The paramount chief gave our ministry fifty acres of land with three abandoned buildings. We have since renovated the buildings and developed the property, dug a well with running water, obtained a power source for electricity, planted trees, and started a cashew farm.

And through the Global Presence Transformation Center, we have established a place of worship and prayer; a vocational school to teach trades to those in the community; the Hope Home for orphans and children at risk; and Hope Academy, the Christian elementary school that has affected the lives of even more children every single day with the amazing truth of God's love. The local community affectionately refers to the Transformation Center as "Hope City."

Two young women, Cassie and Renee (just twenty-eight and eighteen years old at the time), compelled by love and a desire to be part of discipling nations, answered the call from God to be the heart of Jesus in receiving our children into the Hope Home. They poured out three years of their lives as a fragrant offering in Ghana, loving and equipping the children. Renee continues on staff with the Global Presence Hub in Texas, and Cassie is on staff at the Justice House of Prayer in Washington, D.C.

Over the years we have taken many missions teams to Ghana who also loved the children and served the community. And we have conducted numerous equipping schools and raised up local Ghanaian staff, who now run our base there with our continued support and oversight.

It began through hearing the heart of a university student and touching the heart of a king that we have been able to bring great impact to a village and entire region. Transformation involves investing in people's hearts, their identities, and into who God has called them to be.

It is our heart in this book to invest in you, so you can impact the world around you. It all starts from an encounter in which you experience the goodness of God and say yes. Transformation and testimonies can happen in your everyday life, too, when you make love the goal. When you shine brightly, your world will be flipped "upside right" with the love of God.

Compelled by the "Yes" to Go

Rene

Our family was deeply rooted in Wisconsin with our love for God, family, friends, and the redemptive plans over Madison. We had the privilege of standing alongside many people of faith with God's heart and vision for our state. We had seen Him move in love and power time and again on our university campus, in our outreach to the homeless, and in the marketplace.

We were established as a regional hub, having laid apostolic and prophetic foundations. Fiery groups of believers statewide rallied for regional times of worship, prayer, and receiving strategy.

So God's direction for Steven and Elizabeth and me to move to Dallas–Fort Worth, Texas, seemed to come out of left field. But we knew something big was about to happen, for which God needed us to be repositioned.

Just after our house went up for sale on the first weekend of March 2020, the world as we knew it changed. Coronavirus disease 2019 (COVID-19) was declared a pandemic the very next week.

We did not know the magnitude of the changes our world was about to endure. But along with our move to Dallas–Fort Worth came questions for God. How did He see Texas? What were His redemptive purposes for that state?

God spoke to my heart very clearly: *Texas is My anchor state, and I have called you and others to Texas to help secure the anchor.*

I knew this call was not only for our nation but for the nations of the earth. The Bible refers to hope symbolically as an anchor. And the word *anchor* had weight to it, as it anchored my own soul in the midst of a big transition with much uncertainty.

After a significant amount of warfare, we closed on a property in early 2021 that was positioned strategically to tear down demonic altars, to be a place of His presence, to raise up a renaissance company of prophetic artists and musicians, and to release the prophetic destiny of Dallas–Fort Worth as an epicenter of the coming revival.

It does not take masses to do this, just sold-out believers. Several young adults and couples moved to DFW with us out of wholehearted resolve to make an impact for the Kingdom of God. They have opened their hearts to the fire of perfect love to refine and redefine them. We are on the front lines together, advancing God's Kingdom courageously with a continual, unified yes. A company of firebrands is arising!

"I Will Make You Fishers of People"

Steven

In a recent dream, I was dockside in a harbor getting ready to board a beautiful fishing yacht named *Dark Night's Nemesis*. As I read the name, I smiled because I knew we were in for an adventure!

Five of us were ready to board. I was with two anointed Christian leaders, Todd White and Lou Engle, along with the apostle Peter and a Man dressed in white with a beaming, glowing face. I knew it was Holy Spirit. As we boarded the yacht, the Man in white laughed as He pointed at the name of the yacht: *Dark Night's Nemesis*.

"The enemy is in for a rude awakening!" He said. Then He took the helm.

As we left the harbor and headed out to sea, the water was calm as glass.

Peter pointed in a certain direction and said with a big smile, "I remember there being great fishing out there!"

Lou Engle, the lookout, said, "This is a good place for a catch. I can feel it."

So Todd, Peter, and I grabbed a large fishing net and tossed it into the water, and in a moment the net was bulging with a huge catch. We hauled the catch up onto the deck. Then the Man in white said, "Watch this," and laughed again as the catch of fish became people, thrilled to be pulled out of the Sea of Sin.

As we went out even deeper, Lou said, "This is a good place for a catch"—and the same thing happened again.

As each catch was hauled on board, the yacht began supernaturally to grow. Now we were teaching the catch how to catch.

Suddenly the Sea of Sin became tumultuous, and the yacht was tossed to and fro. We were all a bit concerned, but the Man in white laughed and laughed and said, "We are the *Dark Night's Nemesis*, for surely we will overcome this storm in the Sea of Sin. I have crossed these waters many times before, and the chaos always stops." He added in a loud, joy-filled voice, "Be still."

In a moment the seas became calm.

Then we brought on board an even greater catch, because many more people were fishing with us now, using the nets on each side of the yacht. With each catch, the yacht kept growing, to the point that it was now more like a ship, full of people learning how to catch those in the Sea of Sin. They were learning how to release love into the sea to catch those who were in over their heads.

There was joy on deck. Everyone had a part to play to bring in the amazing catches, one after another. As I looked up into the sky, I saw flashes of lightning. The flashes were angels flying overhead, rejoicing over those being rescued from the Sea of Sin.

This dream (see the full interpretation at globalpresence.com /prophetic-pulse) points to the season of God's greatest catch. What started as a small crew of friends going out to make a catch turned into a great and mighty harvest filled with joy and laughter. The Man in white represents Holy Spirit, our Captain and Guide, releasing laughter and joy. The name of the yacht, *Dark Night's Nemesis*, signifies Isaiah 60:1–3:

Arise, shine; for your light has come! And the glory of the Lord is risen upon you. For behold, the darkness shall cover the earth, and deep darkness the people; but the Lord will arise over you, and His glory will be seen upon you. The Gentiles shall come to your light, and kings to the brightness of your rising.

We will be empowered by Holy Spirit to bring awakening into the midst of darkness. It will be a rude awakening to the lost and dying world and to the kingdom of darkness. We are being prepared to bring retribution and vengeance on the enemy through the power and joy of Holy Spirit. We are enforcing the victory of Calvary.

There were five of us who boarded the yacht originally, and this represents grace. There is grace in the midst of shaking for the greatest harvest of sons and daughters. No one is disqualified from participating in this move of Holy Spirit. We will teach those caught in the nets of God's love, and they will be discipled immediately to help bring in the great catch in every sphere of society. There will be room supernaturally for all those rescued from the Sea of Sin to become part of this incredible move.

The Lord is calling all hands on deck to make history for such a time as this. So make yourself ready to receive God's love so that you may love, mend your net, sharpen your sickle, and be ready for an incredible adventure with the Lord. Know that if the Lord is for you, who can be against you? God's angel armies are ready to assist and rejoice with you.

As you finish this book, we commission you to go and make love your goal. Love God with all that you are, and allow Him to love you extravagantly. Then go into all your world and love your neighbors and everyone God puts in your path. You have what it takes. So be strong and courageous and go with boldness and confidence, knowing that God is with you and going before you. The way is being prepared with great joy.

There will be joy in the house of the Lord as it is filled with a bountiful harvest of sons and daughters coming home into the arms of perfect love!

Journey into Perfect Love

Make this declaration to the Lord and yourself:

I declare that I am ablaze with the fire of perfect love. I am awakened to first love, and am compelled to go and release the power of love to my family, to my neighbors, and to the world around me. I am marked to be a burning one, a new breed of firebrand. I am a miracle worker who will heal the sick and raise the dead and cast out demons. I declare that I have eyes to see the harvest of souls that has been set before me, and so I go with boldness, filled with God's love, grace, and power.

Firebrands Arising

One heart, one flame, firebrands are arising
Full of faith, set apart, uncompromising
Branded by the fire of perfect love
Minds set on things above
Tested, found true
They have eyes only for You
Lives laid down
Joyfully casting their crowns
Made ready to meet the Bridegroom
They are consumed

Poem by Rene Springer

ACKNOWLEDGMENTS

We want to thank Renee Toeller, April Bellmore, and Marjorie O'Neal. Each of you played a unique role in proofreading and offering insights on the rough manuscript.

We want to thank David Sluka and Kim Bangs of Chosen Books for giving us this opportunity to publish *The Fire of Perfect Love* and for pursuing us to write this book and make it a reality. Thank you to Jane Campbell for your editing expertise. What a pleasure it was working with you.

To the Global Presence family, you have been on this journey with us into the fiery love of God, and part of many of these supernatural encounters and adventures! Your courageous pursuit of the Lord is an answer to our prayers. We love you.

To our son, Justin, and daughter-in-love, Tina, our beloved grandchildren, and our daughter, Elizabeth: We have learned so much about God's love by being given the privilege to be your parents, Papa and Nene. Our hearts are filled with joy at every stage of life we get to share together. Thank you for your continual encouragement and support of our pursuits. You are all a gift to this world and to our hearts. We love you.

Photos from Steven and Rene's personal library
First Nations photo by Hannah Farrington
Photos of Springer family releasing healing by Matthew Norton

Steven and Rene Springer are the founders and senior leaders of Global Presence Ministries, headquartered in Dallas–Fort Worth, Texas. They are given to the vision of "Bringing God's Presence, Advancing His Kingdom, Transforming Nations." The Springers provide apostolic oversight and encouragement to churches and ministries in the U.S., Africa, and Asia.

The Global Presence Hub in DFW is a community of believers dedicated to personal and societal transformation, centered in God's presence and biblical core values, with demonstrations of God's love, grace, and power. The focus is on equipping, launching, and empowering God's people to "be" the Church, bringing the reality of heaven to earth.

Global Presence also has a ministry base in Ghana, West Africa, called the Transformation Center, which is bringing societal transformation through education at Global Presence Hope Academy, resources for orphaned and at-risk children, academic scholarships, community outreach, and training in vocational skills and Kingdom core values.

Steven and Rene lead the Global Presence Leaders Alliance, a global family of transformational leaders connected relationally to collaborate and strategize in building the Kingdom of God regionally and globally.

On an international level, the Springers collaborate with leaders of government, marketplace, and the Church to disciple nations. Steven and Rene prophesy over and encourage leaders in many spheres of society, including government leaders, top executives in business, and leaders in the arts and entertainment industry of Hollywood.

The Springers have a radical "rags to riches" testimony, since God's unfailing grace saved them while they were in the modeling, fashion, and acting industry, and brought them into the glorious riches of His love. Now they merge their business background and influence in the arts and entertainment industry and the nonprofit sector, empowering the Church to break out of the four walls to bring transformation with the Gospel of the Kingdom.

Steven and Rene are a father and mother in the prophetic, with hearts to raise up the next generation. The Springers have invaluable treasures of insight and experience to impart. They have been invited to help build and establish God's work with other ministries around the world. They have equipped God's people in more than twenty-three nations to prophesy and live a supernatural lifestyle naturally.

The Springers live a supernatural lifestyle with signs and wonders as a regular occurrence. They also train and equip the Church to move in the power of Holy Spirit. They have seen thousands of salvations, deliverances, and miracles, including the lame walking, the blind seeing, the deaf hearing, tumors disappearing, and the dead being raised to life. Whether by "stopping for the one" in everyday life, going hut to hut in Africa, or ministering in large gatherings, the Springers minister faithfully the love and power of God.

Steven and Rene minister individually, as a couple, and as a family with their daughter, Elizabeth, who often travels with them. Their son, Justin, is anointed in the marketplace and has a beautiful wife and children.